HIDDEN HISTORY
of
BRISTOL

HIDDEN HISTORY *of* BRISTOL

Stories from the State Line

V.N. "BUD" PHILLIPS

THE History PRESS

Published by The History Press
Charleston, SC 29403
www.historypress.net

First published 2010

Manufactured in the United States

ISBN 978.1.60949.047.8

Phillips, V. N. (Victor N.)
Hidden history of Bristol : stories from the state line / V.N. "Bud" Phillips.
p. cm.
ISBN 978-1-60949-047-8
1. Bristol (Tenn.)--History--Anecdotes. 2. Bristol (Va.)--History--Anecdotes. 3. Bristol (Tenn.)--Biography--Anecdotes. 4. Bristol (Va.)--Biography--Anecdotes. 5. Bristol (Tenn.)--Social life and customs--Anecdotes. 6. Bristol (Va.)--Social life and customs--Anecdotes. I. Title.
F444.B8P47 2010
976.8'96--dc22
2010033157

Contents

Preface 9
Acknowledgements 11
Introduction: Bristol on the Border 13

Rough and Tumble Days: Bristol's Early History
Chief Smoking Basket and the Rattlers 15
Worse than the Drill: Early Dentistry 17
Dr. Berry's Unusual Remedy 19
Early Form of Shock Treatment: Medical Marvel? 21
How Alabama Street Got Its Name 22
Colonel James King's Well-Traveled Bed 24
Bristol's First Clock Keeps on Ticking 25
Bristol's Prophesying Methuselah 26
Hunger at the Heart of Bristol's First Crime 28

Forgotten Civil War Tales
A Youth Cadet and the Immortal Six Hundred 30
Discovery of Another Civil War Hero 31
Colonel Mosby Comes to Bristol: A Life Before the Gray Ghost of the Confederacy 33
Children of the Confederacy and a Midwife's True Calling 36
Jefferson Davis's Visit to Pleasant Hill 37

Love, Marriage and What Comes After
A Jilted Suitor, a Flying Ham and an Explosive Wedding 40
The Legendary Marrying Parson 42
A Husband's Tribute: The Taj Mahal of Bristol 43
A Chip Saves a Woman from a Poison Cup 45

Mason Jars, Loafers and Swift Justice: The Other Side of Bristol
Moonshine and Mountain Dew on the Streets of Bristol 48
The Big Creek Resort Bubble 49
A Mayor's Swift Justice 51
Loafer's Glory 53
The Only Legal Hanging in Bristol 55

The Women of Bristol
Nora Cross and the Devil's Hideout 57
Annie Goforth Started Bristol's First Laundry 59
Rosetta's Gold 60
The Quest for Rosetta's Gold 63
The Mystery Woman of 1900 64

Presidents, Jokesters, Footloose Majors and Other Characters
Bristol's Forgotten Portrait Painter 67
Chadwick Barr Made the Dead Speak 69
President Andrew Johnson: He Bore the Mark of Bristol 71
The Dancing Major 73
Major Burson and the Watermelon Table 75
The Wild Man of Holston Mountain 77
William G. Lindsey Brought the First Train to Bristol 78
The King of the Bristol Brick Layers 80
Bristol's Famous Cow 81

The African American Community of Bristol
Mercy Hospital Served Bristol's Black Community 84
Slave Quilt Survives in Bristol 86

Ol' Ras Berry 88
The Old Massacre Tree 89
The Incredible Journey 92

Strange and Raucous Happenings
A Bizarre Death in Bristol 94
The Holy Cow and the Reluctant Angel 96
A Mouse Enlivens the Church Service 98

Familiar Places with Hidden Faces
Solar Hill Revisited 101
The Prophecy of Cedar Hill 103
Farewell to Strawberry Field 104
The History of the Mysterious Lot 106
The Christmas Gift House 108

About the Author 111

Preface

The historical articles that appear in this book originally were part of a weekly column published in the *Bristol Herald Courier*, a newspaper operating in Bristol, Virginia. Countless others have contributed in some manner to make possible the work that is presented here. To all of them, whether those who supplied the information, made or supplied pictures, assisted in the actual preparation of the finished manuscript, agreed to and assisted in the publication and who—in any way whatsoever—helped to make this book possible, I extend my deep appreciation. May the best in life be yours.

Acknowledgments

I am unfortunately unable to recall all sources of information for this book since so many individuals were involved, therefore a complete listing of all who contributed would be impossible. Most of them were very old when I arrived here in Bristol in 1953. All have passed away.

A portion of the information used here was more or less common knowledge and was conveyed by several different persons over the years. A small part of the material comes from my own personal recollections. Some who did give me outstanding amounts of information include Ol' Dad Thomas, a noted character of the town in the 1950s and an invaluable resource and wealth of knowledge; Mrs. Minnie Faidley Bridgeman, whose father was Ed Faidley, a pioneer settler of Bristol; Mrs. Allie "Lin" Anderson Blackley, a granddaughter of the founder of Bristol; Aunt Rachel Doyle, old resident here, age ninety-six and still serving as a washer woman when I arrived; Mrs. Betty Scott, a resident who had a knack for remembering everything she ever heard about Bristol; "Brush" Jim Buford, a ninety-seven-year-old born here but a resident of Waco, Texas, and visited Bristol annually; and Mrs. Virginia Seabright Langston, who back in 1953 was old enough to remember the Civil War. Some came from the now long-lost manuscript "A King on Beaver" written in the 1930s by Mrs. Hattie King Taylor, granddaughter of the noted Rev. James King. She died in 1950 so I never met her but the manuscript was priceless.

Mr. Joe Tennis, a close friend and fellow author, made the connection to The History Press. Without him, I would have had no knowledge or contact with all the helpful individuals there. I also wish to extend my gratitude to my friend and coworker, Mr. Bob White, who does everything but make the ideas. I've often said I have the "easy job" of writing. Bob takes over from there. For that, I'm especially grateful.

But whether known or unknown, living or dead: a debt of deeply felt gratitude is extended to them. Without them, this book would have not been possible.

INTRODUCTION

Bristol on the Border

I am told that there are twenty-eight places in America that are known as Bristol. Therefore, let me here identify the city of which I write. This Bristol has a point of distinction in that it is located in two states, Virginia and Tennessee. It was founded in 1852 by Joseph R. Anderson on a tract of land that he had purchased from his father-in-law, Rev. James King. It was founded because the site was destined to become a noted railroad terminal point. At about the same time, Colonel Samuel Goodson, who had done much to bring the railroad here, laid out a town known as Goodsonville that lay north of Beaver Creek. It adjoined the original town of Bristol, Virginia, at that creek. In 1856, due to problems with incorporation, a group of local citizens put the original town of Bristol, Virginia, and adjoining town of Goodsonville together and formed the composite town of Goodson. This was always problematic. The depot had been established in Bristol, Virginia, and, for some reason, the railroad company refused to change the name. Also, for most of the Goodson years, the post office remained as Bristol. Most citizens and business firms continued to use the Bristol name. The problem was solved in 1890 when the Virginia side returned to the name Bristol, was incorporated as such and so remains today. From a small and rather turbulent beginning, Bristol has evolved into the thriving border city that it is today.

Rough and Tumble Days

Bristol's Early History

Chief Smoking Basket and the Rattlers

Most visitors to the historic Deery Inn and its grounds in Blountville, Tennessee, are familiar with a little log cabin known as Colonel King's Ironworks office located behind the inn. Indeed, it was once used as the noted colonel's office, and it was also used as a sleeping room when he needed to stay in the ironworks for a few days. However, it has a little-known pre-King history of which I will share with you here.

According to information handed down through the King and allied families, an Indian known as Chief Smoking Basket appeared seemingly from nowhere at Holly Bend (the name of the original home place on Beaver Creek) sometime around the year 1800. He appeared to be rather old but seemed to have the stamina of a young man. Surprisingly, he also seemed to have a good command of the English language. In time, he also proved to be somewhat of a mystic, having unusual powers to forecast weather and prophesy future events. It seems that his greatest desire was to spend his final years and be buried on the land where he said he was born. To this end, he made a deal with Colonel King. First, he said that there was a buried treasure on the place that he was sure he could find. This he would give to Colonel King for the favors of which he requested.

In those early days, the Bristol knobs were heavily infested with rattlesnakes. For some reason they seemed to be attracted to the King home place at Holly Bend. They often crawled down from the mountains and were frequently

This cabin served as a home for Chief Smoking Basket and later as the office for King Iron Works. Many years ago it was moved to the back yard of the famous Deery Inn in Blountville, Tennessee. *Courtesy of the author.*

found at various places on the home grounds. The slaves were terrorized and this often interfered with their assigned duties. On his first night there, the chief had slept in a vacant slave cabin. On awaking the next morning, he found a giant rattler crawling in under the cabin door. Thus he had a firsthand introduction to the problem. He told Colonel King that he knew a way to rid the area of these dreaded serpents. He would exchange this favor for the previous request of living out his last years and being buried on the old home place.

Colonel King never revealed whether he got the treasure or not, but it is known that he soon bought a large plantation in the Sweetwater Valley section of Tennessee. Family members thought that he bought it with the Indian treasure. The family further told that the chief made plans to fulfill his other consideration with Colonel King in the rattlesnake affair. He soon spent three or four days hunting for particular barks, roots and plants. With all of these, he wove a basket of sorts that family members described as looking somewhat like a hornet's nest. To this he set fire and when it smoldered down into thick billowing smoke he took it and began walking into the forest that then covered the Beaver Knobs. This smoke gave off a sickening, strangling and overpowering odor that could be detected for miles, causing many to want to leave their homes.

Did it work? In 1860, over fifty years later, Rev. King mentioned this strange situation in a letter to his son-in-law, John G. English of Egypt, Mississippi. In that letter, he stated that he never knew of another rattlesnake being found in the knobs after the old chief's smoke walk—or perhaps I should say smoke out.

The chief chose a home site near the confluence of Steele and Beaver Creeks in what is now Rooster Front Park. There, with the aid of the King slaves, he erected a one-room log house. It is known that he did the actual hewing of the logs and the slaves laid them up. There he lived in peace and contentment for several years. He had prophesied that he would die on the day the young James King's first child was born. That child, Sarah, was born February 7, 1813. Chief Smoking Basket died at twilight that evening. He is buried in the King lot in the Ordway Cemetery but he has no marker. A little later, the cabin was moved over to the location that, over a century later, became the site of the Bristol Sewer Plant. When that plant was built, the cabin's future was bleak since it was slated to be demolished. The late Virginia Caldwell saved it from destruction and had it moved to the grounds of the Deery Inn where it may be seen today. It is planned for renovation as soon as funds become available.

Worse than the Drill

Early Dentistry

In the very earliest years of Bristol, there were no dentists. Actually, the medical doctors who were here performed limited dental procedures—mostly the pulling of offending teeth. Largely, that is what most people wanted. If a tooth went bad, then out it came by any means possible. Sometimes the possible means rested on ordinary citizens of a given community, whether or not that person had any medical training. My own grandfather, the late William D. Phillips of Johnson County, Arkansas, pulled teeth for a large community, though I doubt if he ever even saw a medical or dental school in his whole life. Most medical doctors of the time carried tooth pullers as part of their equipment. In the surviving account book of Dr. John J. Ensor, who long lived in what is now the Sesco Building at Cherry and Seventh in Bristol, Tennessee, there is a notation stating that he charged a man 33½

A bout with a local dentist was not only horrific for young John G. English Jr. but proved to be horrific for the dentist. *Courtesy of the author.*

cents for extracting what he called "an oppressive tooth." I have often wondered what the ½ cent was for.

The first actual dentist to set up practice in Bristol was Dr. John Keys, and he was both a dentist and medical doctor. However, he seemed to have preferred the practice of dentistry. (He is not to be confused with another John Keys, who married the widow of Dr. B.F. Zimmerman, Bristol's first medical doctor.)

Other dentists soon came and set up practice in this city. By 1900, there were several of them here.

Dentistry was a much dreaded procedure in those early days. So much so that one dentist, Dr. Wilbar, advertised in a local paper that his work was "less horrific than others." Another dentist, Dr. Grant, had a horrific experience himself while pulling a badly infected tooth. Colonel John G. English, a son-in-law of the noted Rev. James King, had a twenty-one-year-old son, John English Jr., who had suffered excruciating pain for two or three days when Dr. Grant was called in. Colonel English recorded the "rest of the story" in his diary in his own peculiar way of expressing things.

> *He* [Dr. Grant] *got Johnny on the bed and got hold of the bad tooth with his pullers and gave a yank, but it hurt so bad that John came up with the pullers, thus to no avail. Then the doctor had me to hold down his head and put my servant, Jabaz, on his feet. Then the doctor got up on the bed and straddled him about the waist. He then applied the pullers with much trouble since the boy could hardly stand for his mouth to be touched. It was so sore and tender. But a hard and fast jerk brought the tooth out. Johnny*

> *seemed then to swoon and lay moaning for a moment. Then he suddenly leaped up with such force that we were all knocked loose. Dr. Grant was violently knocked backward over the foot of the bed and landed flat on his back in the floor with his feet high in the air. His head hit hard on the floor and bounced, thus he lay addled a little while. The pullers were thrown and hit Jabaz in the stomach that curled him up double for a time. Johnny jumped out of the bed and ran wildly around the room leaping and yelling and then took out to the kitchen still yelling with blood coming out of his mouth. This scared the cook so bad that she screamed and ran up the back yard and up to the orchard before she stopped. Some of the food burned for which I chided her much. Dr. Grant finally got up and started to leave but he had much trouble trying to mount his horse for his back hurt so bad and he was somewhat injured in the straddles for Johnny leaping up fast and hard under him during the first try.*

Colonel English then wrote that he paid Dr. Grant one dollar, a hard earned dollar indeed!

When Johnny was finally caught, he was given a double dose of Dr. Scales's Pain Reliever, a remedy that was later found to be pure whiskey with a disguised odor. The colonel wrote that the boy then slept for fourteen hours without waking. Alas, poor Johnny died about a year later, but not from dental troubles. Today he sleeps in an unmarked grave in our historic East Hill Cemetery.

Now, reader, aren't you thankful for modern dentistry?

Dr. Berry's Unusual Remedy

Dr. H.T. Berry was among the several doctors who began their Bristol practices in the immediate post-Civil War era. He soon had a considerable number of devoted patients. Along with his medical success, he also became a highly respected citizen and was very active in social and civic affairs.

When Sullins College was founded, he was among the first to be selected to serve on its official board. In spite of his busy schedule, he also found time to be an active partner in a local mercantile establishment.

His prosperity soon reached the point where he could take up residence with the rail-view crowd—this was the name given to that group of select citizens who could afford homes on Third Street in Bristol, Tennessee, and Washington Street in Bristol, Virginia (then called Goodson). These were

Dr. H.T. Berry had an unusual but effective cure for hiccups. In one case, it made an enemy of his patient. *Courtesy of the author.*

two of the most elite streets in the city. Both had views of the railroad, and to be able to live on those streets was considered to be a status symbol at that time. Dr. Berry had both his home and office on Third Street. Both were demolished long ago to make room for a development by the Stone Lumber Company.

Another early citizen living here at that time was John N. Bosang. Mr. Bosang arrived in Bristol about 1854 and became the new town's first saloonkeeper. He was considered to be a rather savage man. He was always heavily armed and his home was practically an armed fortress. Many in the town feared him. He and his wife, Lucinda B. Bosang, long lived in a modest house on Spencer Street. They became patients of Dr. Berry.

In late September 1868, Mr. Bosang was seized with a prolonged spell of hiccups. After two days of almost constant hiccupping, Dr. Berry was sent for. It was well-known that this doctor was good at finding unusual remedies for persistent ailments. After what appeared to be some deep thought, he took from his black bag a bottle of white powder and prescribed the dosage. Then he rode away.

But while not a block away, he whirled his horse and raced up to the gate calling to Mr. Bosang and asking him if he had taken any of the medicine. The startled patient replied that indeed he had—and a double dose at that. In seeming horror, the good doctor blurted out that he had accidentally given him a deadly poison and that he would be dead in a few minutes. At that, the terrified patient began running around the yard, begging the doctor to save him. Dr. Berry let this go on for a few minutes and then asked Mr. Bosang where his hiccups had gone. Indeed, they had ceased. He then—

laughing all the while—told him that he had lied about the poison, but that he had just scared the hiccups out of him.

Mr. Bosang didn't find it funny at all. He became very angry, refused to pay the bill and would never speak to Dr. Berry again.

But angry as he was, he had to admit that the remedy had worked!

Early Form of Shock Treatment: Medical Marvel?

I often make the comment that if a thing can happen, it has happened in Bristol. The more I research local history, the more I am convinced that this is true. Good, bad, in-between, far out, almost unheard of—you name it—it has happened in Bristol!

This very depressed woman received an unusual form of shock treatment. It worked but the form of treatment made her very angry. *Courtesy of the author.*

It is not well-known that an early form of shock treatment for depression took place here in Bristol. One treatment is all I know about, but apparently it worked.

Earl Browder came here from near Plum Branch, South Carolina, to work as a typesetter for I.C. Fowler, editor of the *Bristol News*. He was a widower when he arrived here but soon married a widow, Sadie Longsworth Smith. Her late husband had been killed in a Civil War battle. Since that sad event, she had been chronically depressed. Sometimes she would sit for days just staring into space. Other times, she had violent temper fits, during which she made life unbearable for poor Earl. She had been to every doctor then practicing in Bristol. Alas, the tranquilizers and antidepressants we now have were not then available. So, she grew steadily worse.

One day while reviewing the papers on the exchange table at the *Bristol News*, Mr. Browder read a brief news article concerning how a man in Illinois cured his wife's deep depression. In desperation, he decided to try that strange treatment on his wife.

Securing ice from Thomas C. Lancaster's ice pit, he put it in a large pail of water. At home he found his wife sitting in the shade of a large tree, head bowed, eyes closed and lost in the depths of paralyzing morbid, sad thoughts.

Mr. Browder slipped up behind her and quickly dashed the icy water over her head and shoulders. Though she had hardly moved or spoken a word in several days, she sprang up and shouted curses and obscenities, jumped, kicked and ran circles around the shade tree. Seeing her husband standing with the empty pail in his hand and not making much effort to conceal his mirth, she charged directly at him. Then, and as Ol' Dad Thomas used to say, "That quare woman fit [fought] him all over the yard and out into the street."

Apparently, that one treatment did the trick. She was quite normal for the rest of her life.

HOW ALABAMA STREET GOT ITS NAME

Until 1872, the area around the route of present-day Alabama Street was part of one of the choice grain fields on the plantation of John G. King. The plantation was then known by two names: King Spring or Oakland, most commonly known by the latter name.

King had inherited the vast acreage after the death of his father, the Reverend James King who died in July 1867. In 1872, John King had a large portion of the land laid off into streets and lots to meet the demand of fast-growing Bristol for more residential space.

Prior to this time, he had built a large, white-columned mansion on a hill overlooking the noted King Spring. This original mansion has long since burned, but the site is near what is now DeFriece Park and is occupied by a newer dwelling, now the home of Tom Davenport.

When King's first addition to Bristol was laid off, he planned a grand avenue, leading from the town of Bristol and extending to this fine country estate. This was to be known as King Avenue, but the proposed name was later changed.

Soon after the Civil War, a family of ex-slaves arrived here from Alabama; the family name was Cane. That family became tenants of the southern portion of John King's plantation (near present-day Cedar Valley Road). The first child born to that family after their arrival here was a little girl. They named her Alabama in honor of their native state. Almost daily, the father of this family came to the King mansion to assist in the work there. One day he left, promising to return first thing the next morning. But he did not arrive the next morning.

Several days passed and still he did not come. It was then that King became concerned and rode down on horseback to check on him. When he arrived at the Cane place, he was greeted with a pitiful sight. Little Alabama Cane was crying and vainly trying to milk the family cow. She told King that all the others in her family had gone to bed and would not get up for three days now. She had been without food all the while. She was only five years old.

King immediately rushed into the house to find all the family members dead, both her parents and two siblings. Some sickness had befallen them or, as some doctors thought, their deaths had been caused by food poisoning. King lifted the frightened little girl up onto his saddle and quickly rode home. There he placed her in the care of his kind wife, Harriett King. Neighbors returned to the site of the horrible tragedy and buried the remaining Cane family in the lower King slave burial ground.

Having been rescued by King, the child would hardly let him out of her sight. He became very fond of her as well. When he was having his first addition of Bristol laid off, he would often take her with him and place her under a large sycamore tree to play while he directed surveyors in their work. The King family became very fond of this little girl and took her into their home. There she lived until she married. The late Mrs. Melinda "Aunt Lin" Owen, a daughter of John G. King, often spoke fondly of this little orphan girl who was raised in her family home and in telling the whole story, would often become misty-eyed.

Late one afternoon, after directing the work for his first addition, it suddenly occurred to King that he should honor the orphan child by naming a street for her. The grand King Avenue he had planned would now be named Alabama Street and thus we have that street today.

In time, this became one of the most elite streets in Bristol, Tennessee. It should be noted that another street did bear the King name for several years. We know it as Sixth Street.

COLONEL JAMES KING'S WELL-TRAVELED BED

Often, a relic pertaining to a pioneer resident of a given locality may remain there for several generations after that person is gone. Sometimes that article may change hands several times and be moved about within the area until its earliest owners become virtually unknown. Often they end up in an attic, shed or barn or, worse still, in a trash dump. Some are rescued and again become highly valued heirlooms by grateful new owners. Such is the story of Colonel James King's bed.

The story of this bed begins in Sullivan County, Tennessee, at Holly Bend, the plantation home of Revolutionary War colonel James King. Colonel King came to this area and settled in Beaver Creek five miles from what is now downtown Bristol in the last quarter of the eighteenth century. As was the case with many larger plantations, Holly Bend had its own furniture shop. The difference here was that at least one slave was trained in the trade of cabinetmaking at Mount Vernon. This shop stood between the main house and Beaver Creek, just above the large spring that long provided water for the plantation. In the back was a room dedicated to coffin making and foreshadows a very interesting story to be told in this column later. The shop not only made furniture for this plantation but Col. King was known to have sold pieces to pioneer settlers all over the area. It is thought that many of these pieces still remain, but alas, they were not marked.

In many old estate inventories of the period, in the possession of this writer, bedsteads always were valued more than any other article in the house. Such is the case today as ornate poster beds are rarely offered cheaply. In the case of Colonel King, the bed he had made for himself was custom fitted for his frame and statue. Of solid cherry construction, it was often told that it was made from the tree that shaded the cabinetmaker's shop. Lightning had struck and killed the tree, and the high, soaring bed posts were turned into one piece from this wood and stood nine feet tall.

The bed was used by Colonel King until he died on August 17, 1825. After his death, it came into the possession of his son Rev. James King and was long used in his fine brick home standing at what is now 54 King Street in Bristol, Virginia. During the time it was in Rev. King's possession, it was sometimes used by Andrew Jackson when he stopped here to visit on his way to and from Washington D.C. Older family members often referred to it as the Jackson Bed. At Rev. King's death in 1867, it passed to Joseph R. Anderson and his wife, who was the granddaughter of Colonel King. When Joseph Anderson built his fine new home in 1881, he bought mostly new furnishings for it. At that time, the old bed was given to Nehemiah Strange, a former slave of the Andersons. Nehemiah soon moved to Greene County, Tennessee, and took the bed with him. Almost seventy-five years later, I heard of this bed through a great-great-granddaughter of Colonel James King. She gave me enough clues that I went searching for it. After two or three trips to Greene County, I located the old bed. It was then in a chicken house and had been used as a roost for decades. I was able to save it from sure destruction and brought it home to Pleasant Hill. There it remained for many years until it was purchased by a descendant of Colonel James King's only daughter, and it is being proudly displayed on Richland Avenue in Nashville, Tennessee.

Bristol's First Clock Keeps on Ticking

Old Pleasant Hill, where I have long lived, is virtually a museum. It is filled with relics of the past, many of which pertain to early Bristol. Among the most treasured relics here is an old clock that was ticking away a few years before the founding of Bristol. It was a gift to Joseph R. Anderson and Malinda King Anderson on the occasion of their wedding, which was held June 13, 1845. It was given by Malinda's father, the Reverend James King. (He presented a clock as a wedding gift to each of his children.) The clock that Rev. King gave the young couple was a weight-powered ogee model made by Elisha Manross in Bristol, Connecticut. King made the purchase in Abingdon from Greenway's mercantile at a cost of $2.75. It was set up and put to running by a close friend of the Andersons, future president Andrew Johnson, who had attended the wedding and remained for a few days afterward.

Soon after the wedding, the Andersons moved into what we now know as the Anderson Town House in Blountville. This clock graced the mantel there until the move was made to Bristol in 1853. Here it was put on the mantel in the new Anderson home and became the first clock in the new town.

In 1881, Mr. Anderson built his palatial home at 516 Anderson Street. At that time, he put new clocks on the mantels in the principal rooms. He gave the old weight clock to Nehemiah Strange, a former slave of the Andersons, who long served as a hired servant long after the war. Mr. Strange soon moved to Greene County, Tennessee, taking the old clock with him.

Though this clock had long been gone from Bristol when I arrived here in 1953, it was not forgotten. A granddaughter of Joseph Anderson gave

This clock, long the property of J.R. Anderson, founder of Bristol, became the first to be used in his new town. It is now owned by Bob White, co-producer of this book. *Courtesy of Bob White.*

me enough information that I was able to trace it down. When finally found, it was in a dark old smokehouse that stood in the backyard of the house of the former slave's great-granddaughter in Greene County, Tennessee. The dial side of that old clock was flat against the wall on a high shelf and could have been easily missed by those who didn't have a keen interest in finding it. Surprisingly, after 161 years, this first clock in Bristol is in good condition, both case and works, and keeps time with my best watch.

It is my duty as town historian to pass all things important to Bristol's history on to the next generation for safekeeping. I decided this relic was one of the most important and, upon the occasion of a wedding anniversary, I released the clock to the care of Bob and Michelle White who have many children. It is my hope that it will handed down through the generations.

Bristol's Prophesying Methuselah

It is not generally known that there lived in early Bristol a slave who was reputed to be the oldest man in the world. He was Silas "Old Si" Goodson, who was born in Maryland about 1730–32.

Old Si Goodson was noted for his accurate prophesies and was reputed to be the oldest man in the world. His powder horn still exists, indicating he was a much-trusted slave. *Courtesy of the author.*

He later came into the possession of Major Thomas Goodson of what is now Floyd County, Virginia. Major Goodson was the common ancestor of all the Goodsons now living in this area. Major Goodson gave him to a daughter, Sarah, wife of Colonel James King of the iron works fame, in what is now the Bristol area. Silas eventually passed to a son of this family, the Reverend James King, who owned the land where downtown Bristol is now located.

By the time he came into this latter family, he was more than a century old and had become a much beloved, highly respected and much privileged slave. For one thing, he was allowed the use of a gun for hunting purposes. He was also allowed a special diet that he thought helped him to stay young. This included a mixture of honey and buttermilk and plenty of acorns. He also believed that a daily dip in cold water helped along this line. For years he did this in Beaver Creek at a point directly in front of what is now the Bristol Public Library. He chose that place because a cold spring flowed into the creek there. This was his daily routine—even if he had to break ice to do so. He also slept in the open air the year around.

For as long as he lived, he continued to do hard work on the King plantation. It was long told that on his 110th birthday, he split and laid up

100 fence rails. But what really caused him to be long remembered was his seeming ability to prophecy future events. He foretold the death at sea of Rev. King's son, William. He also said that the winter of 1856–57 would be the coldest ever known some 12 years prior to that actually happening.

Then, in 1842, he arose one morning and told that in a dream he had seen a large city spreading over the bit meadow and fields where downtown Bristol is now located. Rev. King recorded this prophecy in his diary under the date August 1, 1842. On August 1, 1852, Old Si—then about 120 years old— helped the surveyors lay out the city he had envisioned.

On May 3, 1862, Old Si spent the morning digging roots for medicine making. Later that day, a band of bushwhackers raided the King home place. Old Si grabbed his gun and went in hot pursuit of them. It was too much for his aging heart. He dropped dead on the lot where now stands the Belvedere mansion, back of Tenth Street in Bristol, Tennessee.

He was buried in the slave section of East Hill Cemetery.

HUNGER AT THE HEART OF BRISTOL'S FIRST CRIME

In every city—indeed in every location—there are places where firsts have occurred. There are many such places here in Bristol. Here, I will write of Bristol's first crime.

In late 1853, John H. Moore of Russell County, Virginia, contracted to buy Lot 164 in Bristol, Virginia. Upon that lot he soon opened the first store on the Virginia side of town. The store, a frame building, stood on the northwest corner of Lee and Main (now State) Streets. During the cold February winter of 1854, Bristol's first-known crime was committed in—or under, which is more exact—this store building.

In those early days, when Bristol was barely a village, many poor families moved here hoping to better their economic conditions a bit. Unfortunately, some of them didn't do so well. One such family lived in a small rental house near the east side of the railroad yard (a block or so northeast of our present depot). The father of that family had found no steady work by which he could support his large family. Thus, during that very cold and snowy February, the family became nearly destitute.

John H. Moore had a wooden barrel of molasses sitting flat on the floor in the grocery section of his general store. During a raging snowstorm, the father of the destitute family slipped quietly through the dead of night and crawled under the store building. Using an auger, he bored two holes through the floor before he finally hit the bottom of the molasses barrel. He filled two tin pails, but there was no way to stop the flow. The rest of the molasses was lost in the dirt under the floor.

Mr. Moore found the holes in the floor the next morning and soon was able to detect what had happened. Jesse Aydlotte, who was then acting as the town constable, was summoned. Locating the thief was not difficult. One of the tin pails evidently had a hole in its bottom. Mr. Aydlotte simply followed the trail of drips in the snow to the little house over beyond the tracks. There he found the hungry family shivering around a crude table wolfing down molasses along with cold cornbread. It was then that mercy overcame justice.

Instead of arresting the poor man, Mr. Aydlotte gave him a job. Further, he went back to Moore's store and had more food sent to the destitute family. And in fairness to Mr. Moore, it should be told that he generously donated some of that food. Such were the golden hearts that beat within the breasts of many a pioneer Bristolian.

Under the patient guidance of Mr. Aydlotte, this poor man became a master carpenter. In time, he built his own nice home in what was then an elite section of Bristol. He has descendants here now—some of who are fairly well known.

No, I won't identify them for you. After all, who wants the first thief in Bristol as an ancestor?

Further, I should tell you that the kind Mr. Aydlotte who allowed mercy to triumph over justice was the driving force behind the organization of our great State Street Methodist Church.

Forgotten Civil War Tales

A Youth Cadet and the Immortal Six Hundred

It is not generally known that the last survivor of the youth cadets who fought in the noted Civil War Battle of New Market on May 15, 1864, is buried in Bristol's historic East Hill Cemetery.

He was William Morrison "Uncle Billy" Wood, who was born in 1846 at Old Pleasant Hill in Scott County, Virginia. Soon after the close of the Civil War, he came to Bristol and, here, successfully engaged in merchandising and a bit of banking. For years he appeared to be a confirmed bachelor. However, that all changed when Mrs. Lavina Haden McClellan, a widow, came here from Mississippi to see her daughter through school. He married this young widow and they soon moved into the brick house that still stands at 332 Sixth Street. In later years, this house served as the offices for Dr. J.L. McCord. It is now historically marked as the Billy Wood house.

Billy Wood had four brothers, all of whom served in the Civil War and all finally came to live in Bristol. All were buried in East Hill Cemetery. However, one was later moved to Glenwood.

Uncle Billy long survived his wife. He was an avid sports fan and was very active in local, social and civic functions up to near the end of his long life.

When he was in his midnineties he gave the principal address at the VMI commemoration of the battle in which he fought when he was but seventeen years old.

William "Billy" Wood became the last survivor of the youth cadets who fought in the Battle of New Market. *Courtesy of the author.*

This last survivor of those youth cadets died in 1943 at Old Hickory. He was ninety-seven years old. The burial site and monument of this noted Bristolian may be seen at the south side of Hugh Hagan Drive in our historic East Hill Cemetery.

Discovery of Another Civil War Hero

As another interesting note, extensive research on our historic East Hill Cemetery has recently revealed that near Billy Wood is buried one of the Immortal Six Hundred.

During the Civil War, military prisons for both the Union and Confederacy became very overcrowded. This led to inhumane conditions for the prisoners. Disease and outright starvation became rampant in those prisons. Heat in summer and cold in winter added to their already miserable conditions. Reports of the suffering being endured by prisoners of this war inflamed the feelings and created a desire for retaliation on both sides. The inability to take cities, such as Charleston, South Carolina, became very frustrating to the Union. This caused Union leaders such as Quincy A. Gilmore and J.G. Foster to continually bomb that city. General Samuel Jones made an effort to lessen these attacks by housing two separate units of Federal prisoners within Charleston. Then Union general Foster sent for an equal number of Confederate prisoners from Fort Delaware to be placed on the beach in front of the Union batteries located on Morris Island, South Carolina. This group of six hundred Confederates eventually became known as the Immortal Six Hundred.

An epidemic of yellow fever soon broke out in Charleston. This caused all soldiers to be removed. The remaining 520 Confederates (of the original six hundred) were taken to Fort Pulaski where several more of the group died. On March 5, 1865, the remaining prisoners were moved back to Fort Delaware. One of the survivors of the Immortal Six Hundred was Robert C. Bryan, who was born February 11, 1842, in Washington County, Virginia. He was a son of Landon Calvin and Dorcas Lintecum Bryan. His grandfather was James Bryan, an early pioneer–settler in the area of Meadowview, Virginia.

While in the Confederate service, Robert C. Bryan was made a lieutenant and later became a captain. After the war ended, he returned to his Virginia home. A little over three years later, on December 31, 1868, he was married to Caroline Matilda Hunter, who was born February 22, 1849, on a farm near Jonesborough, Tennessee. She was a daughter of Linville and Matilda Hunter. Her parents had moved from near Jonesborough to Meadowview, Virginia, and it was there she met Captain Bryan. The couple lived for a short time near Meadowview. Their first child was born there. By 1872, they were living in Louisville, Kentucky, where Mr. Bryan had become a tobacco trader. Two more sons were born there. After 1875—likely about 1883—they moved to Bristol. Bristol, at that time, had become a thriving and fast-growing town. It offered many opportunities for those who sought to improve their lot in life. That is likely why the Bryans came here. In 1896, the family was living at 42 Fourth Street. At that time, he and his two sons were listed as clerks. By 1908, a move had been made to 310 Pennsylvania. Captain Bryan died there on February 11, 1912. He is buried in Section Three of Bristol's historic East Hill Cemetery. His widow lived until December 22, 1933. Her last years were spent with her only daughter, Dora Belle Bryan McClanahan-Francis at 400 Taylor Street in Bristol, Tennessee.

Captain Bryan and his wife only had three children. Dora Belle (the only daughter and oldest child) married James McClanahan and later Olin E.

Francis. William E. Bryan, the oldest son, married Ollie E. Mayes and was a Bristol businessman until his death in 1929; his widow survived him by forty-five years and died here in 1974. The youngest son, Samuel Bryan, never married; he became a traveling salesman and died in Charleston, West Virginia, in 1948. It is thought that he is buried here in the Bryan family lot but there is no marker for his grave.

There may be others of the Immortal Six Hundred buried in our cemetery, but I have no knowledge of them.

Colonel Mosby Comes to Bristol

A Life Before the Gray Ghost of the Confederacy

Captain Joseph W. Owen, born February 27, 1835, was long a well-known and highly respected citizen of Bristol. He was well connected since he was a close relative of Rev. James King and Colonel Samuel E. Goodson. His mother died when he was a child. Her dying request to her cousin, Colonel Goodson, was for him to take and raise her children, Joseph W. Owen, James G. Owen and their sister, Martha Jane Owen. A baby girl in this family, Margaret King Owen, was dropped by her nurse and died of the injuries before the death of the mother. With the aid of a slave nurse and a cook, Goodson brought these children to adulthood in wealth and good health.

When Captain Owen was about twenty, he went to old Mexico with the intention of settling there. He engaged in the business of buying horses and mules at very cheap prices and then selling them to early settlers in Texas for a handsome profit. In this, he was doing very well. However, Colonel Goodson persuaded him to come back to this area to aid him in his several business pursuits. He arrived back here in February 1857. Later that month, he assisted in the first burial that became the East Hill Cemetery. It was on his word that we establish the date of this very historic burial ground.

According to his daughters, it was Captain Owen who persuaded the noted colonel John S. Mosby to settle in Bristol. He was a distant cousin to Mosby. Mosby was on his way to Memphis to open a law practice there, but he stopped to visit these relatives and was persuaded to stay put in Bristol. Some say that another strong incentive is that he was running out of money.

During the Civil War, Joseph Owen served with Colonel Mosby and his Raiders. He distinguished himself in several engagements of that group. He was highly valued as a close advisor to Colonel Mosby.

John S. Mosby spent almost three years practicing law in Bristol and then went away to serve in the Civil War. For years, his likeness was displayed on a prominent corner in downtown Bristol. *Courtesy of the author.*

On December 7, 1864, while on a furlough here, Owen married Alice Margaret King, a daughter of Cyrus King and granddaughter of the noted reverend James King. The ceremony had barely ended when Captain Owen had to flee out the back door to escape an approaching group of Federals. He did not see his bride again for over a month. A son of this marriage was Samuel G. Owen, who settled in Birmingham, Alabama. He was twice married but left no descendents. Captain Owen's first wife died August 14, 1887. He soon married her first cousin Melinda "Linnie" King, daughter of John G. and Harriet Netherland King. Doubtless, several of my readers will remember his two lovely daughters, Hattie and Reveley Owen, who long lived at 237 Solar Street.

At the death of Colonel Samuel Goodson on January 31, 1870, Captain Owen inherited the larger part of his estate and thus became one of the richest men in Bristol. His cousin, Colonel Mosby, was never much liked in Bristol. After the war, when he became associated with Ulysses S. Grant, he became the brunt of severe dislike and criticism. This greatly troubled Captain Owen, who was always on the defensive for his cousin. During the height of that furor, he had an image of Mosby carved in marble. This he attached to the side of a bank building that stood on the northeast corner of Lee and Main (State) Streets. It remained there for years and was then taken down when that building was demolished around 1900. It remained in Bristol until a few years ago.

For several years, Captain Owen and his family lived at 611 Locust Street. While living there, his neighbor, John H. Caldwell, began extensive remodeling of the old David Ensor house into the grand mansion that now is the present Weaver Funeral Home.

On May 13, 1907, Captain Owen and his two young daughters were standing in the street as the front columns of that grand mansion were being put into place. His daughter, Hattie, remembered that when the first column (the one on the east side) was being put into place, her father suddenly fell dead at her feet. He was buried in the Cyrus King lot in our historic East Hill Cemetery.

As for Mosby, he practiced law in Bristol for almost three years after coming here in December 1858. He managed to rent on credit the former little two-room building that had been used as an office by Dr. B.F. Zimmerman. This building stood slightly east of the present northeast corner of Lee and State Streets. He used the front room as his office and made his living quarters in the back room. However, he did not have nor could he afford a bed on which to sleep. Austin M. Appling, an early Bristol merchant, gave him an old poster bed that he had recently replaced. In fact, he had placed this old bed in his woodshed intending to chop it into firewood. Mosby slept on this bed through the remainder of his time in Bristol. It was discovered years later and purchased by this writer; it was later moved to Ben Bolt, a private residence in Tazewell, Virginia.

A myth has developed that he returned here after the Civil War and resumed his law practice. It is further believed that he continued to live in Bristol until he died and was buried here—but none of this is true. In fact, he was not back in Bristol but a very few times. One of those times was shortly before he died. A local group, headed by Colonel Samuel L. King, engaged him to come here and deliver a speech. For this he was to be paid an ample fee. However, for some reason, he was not paid.

One of the last letters Mosby wrote was a request to Colonel Samuel King for this fee, but apparently his request was not filled.

A very modest stone marks his grave. It is located in the old town cemetery at Warrenton in Fauquier County, Virginia. Very often I receive calls asking how to find Mosby's grave in East Hill Cemetery here in Bristol. Unfortunately, I have to tell them that it is not here. He died in Warrenton on May 30, 1906.

CHILDREN OF THE CONFEDERACY AND A MIDWIFE'S TRUE CALLING

During the early years and well into the twentieth century, Bristol had several older women who practiced midwifery. Among the better known and most successful of these was Aunt Polly Taylor.

She and her husband, Dawson Taylor, had moved to Bristol from Pennsylvania in 1857. Within a short time, her reputation as a highly skilled midwife was well established. Even local doctors often sought her assistance in difficult cases.

On July 10, 1864, Liza Rhea Netherland Brewer, wife of local merchant W.P. Brewer, went into a very difficult labor with twins. Dr. Richard M. Coleman, who had been called to the Brewer residence on Third Street, finally decided it was time to send for Aunt Polly.

Aunt Polly Taylor was an early midwife of early Bristol. She found a unique way of going against her husband's orders not to deliver Rebel babies. *Courtesy of the author.*

The Taylors lived a few blocks away on Virginia Street. When one of the Brewer servants arrived at the Taylor home, a little problem developed. Though Aunt Polly was willing to go, her husband would not give his consent—he indeed forbade her to go.

The town was then strongly divided over the Civil War. Mr. Taylor was a rabid Unionist while the Brewers had sided with the Confederacy. "Let the damned rebels die, there's too many of them around here now," Mr. Taylor had shouted at Aunt Polly.

The kind old midwife pretended to meekly obey, but she had a calling that knew no political divisions; she was fully determined to find a way to be true to her calling. Shortly, she told her husband that she would go next door to visit Mrs. Bosang. Once there, she asked her neighbor's husband, John Bosang, for a bottle of the strongest whiskey he had on hand (he was a local saloonkeeper). With it, she hastened back home and told her husband that Mr. Bosang had sent him a little gift. "It's very mild," she added, "You'll have to drink a lot of it to do you any good."

That was not hard for old Dawson Taylor to do. Immediately, he consumed an ample portion of his neighbor's "gift." Within a few minutes, he was out cold. Aunt Polly then hastened off to the Brewer home.

Shortly, she safely delivered a healthy boy and girl and was back home long before her husband knew she was gone.

One of the twins was James King Brewer, long a prominent Bristol businessman, who built the lovely old home that still stands at 220 Johnson Street in Bristol, Virginia. The other twin was Harriett, or Hattie, who became the wife of Dr. Joseph S. Bachman. Healthy they must have been.

Mrs. Bachman died April 26, 1953, at the age of eighty-nine; Mr. Brewer died in 1954 at the age of ninety. Mrs. Bachman was the great-grandmother of widely known Bristol physician Dr. Bennett Y. Cowan Jr.

Jefferson Davis's Visit to Pleasant Hill

Pleasant Hill at 214 Johnson Street in Bristol, Virginia, has welcomed many visitors during the 134 years it has stood high on Solar Hill, overlooking downtown Bristol. None of them have been better known than Jefferson Davis, the only president of the Confederate States of America.

Captain J.H. Wood had become a friend of Mr. Davis around 1856. The two stayed in touch through the Civil War years that soon followed. J.H. Wood became a captain in the Confederate army during the war. In

When Jefferson Davis visited Pleasant Hill in Bristol, Virginia, on August 22 and 23, 1873, he slept in the north (right) upstairs bedroom of this historic home. *Courtesy of the author.*

1867, Captain Wood came to Bristol where he began a long and successful law career.

In 1872, he erected his large, new home on the newly subdivided Solar Hill. He named his home in honor of the old Pleasant Hill in Scott County, Virginia, where he was born and reared.

Near midnight on August 21, 1873, Jefferson Davis, who was on his way home after an eastern visit, arrived at the Bristol depot. He spent the rest of the night at the nearby Virginia House Hotel. At that time, John G. Wood, a brother of Captain Wood, operated the hotel.

Early the next morning, the distinguished guest was taken to Pleasant Hill for a visit with his highly valued friend. Though he had planned to leave Bristol on a late afternoon train, Captain Wood persuaded him to spend the night. It was long told in the family that Mr. Davis and Captain Wood sat in the north parlor and talked far into the night—so long that candles had to be replaced before they retired for the evening. It's doubtless that their conversation centered on the late war. Davis slept in the north upstairs bedroom.

Though Mr. Davis had intended to keep his visit more or less a secret, word soon spread that he was at Pleasant Hill. Before breakfast was finished, a very large crowd had assembled in front of the house. At the insistence of that crowd, Mr. Davis delivered a short speech from the front portico (the present large porch had not been added). Ol' Dad Thomas, then sixteen, was yet living when I arrived in Bristol. He stood nearby during the speech and could quote long portions of it.

The Wood family never forgot that visit and would never let anyone else forget it either. None of that family now lives here, but the old home still stands. It is indeed a pleasant home for this writer.

Love, Marriage and What Comes After

A Jilted Suitor, a Flying Ham and an Explosive Wedding

The claim made in the title of this article may be rightly taken as a matter of opinion, but I think those who were there would have agreed with me. Certainly none of them ever forgot it.

When I arrived here nearly seventy years later, five or six of those who were in attendance at that wedding were still living, including the maid of honor. They all gave vivid details of the most unusual and certainly unexpected turn of events during the exchange of vows of the solemn ceremony.

Judson Ebersohl (some pronounced his name Eversole) moved his family here in 1881 from around Harrisonburg in Rockingham County, Virginia. Already a wealthy merchant, he opened a store on the south side of the first block of Moore north of present State. A little farther up the block, he rented a fine brick house for his home. His intention was to build an even finer house farther up the street, but his plans changed on that never-to-be-forgotten wedding day.

Mr. Ebersohl's first wife died within a month after the family moved here. She rests in an unmarked grave in East Hill Cemetery. Shortly after he became a widower, he began a courtship with Melcenie Seabright, whose family lived on Fourth Street on the Tennessee side of Bristol. The courtship soon became intense but the stern father of the sixteen-year-old girl refused to let her marry the thirty-two-year-old widower until she became eighteen.

Sometimes Bristol weddings were more exciting than expected. This was the case when a jilted suitor turned to explosives to vent his anger. Pictured here is the groom, who was felled by a flying ham. *Courtesy of the author.*

The wedding day was set for the day she reached that age—December 24, 1883.

The wedding day was mild enough for the large windows of the Ebersohl parlor to be open as the couple stood before the Reverend George A. Caldwell to be married. Just as Rev. Caldwell began the exchange of vows, there was a thunderous explosion that demolished the large well-filled smoke house out back. Debris and various cuts of meat, including large bins of sausage, went flying everywhere. A large ham sailed through the open window, hit the groom in his back and sent him sprawling forward. He, in turn, knocked Rev. Caldwell backward to the floor and went down on all fours astride him. The large ham was still on his back but he soon bucked it off, as one present later told me. There was a barrel of eggs in that smoke house. Shattered and mixed with gobs of sausage, they splattered over several of the guests.

The bride also went down in a faint and, when revived, fled the room screaming. It was later learned that a jilted suitor of hers, who had vowed to stop her wedding, set off the explosion. He left town that day and was never seen here again.

He had created a wedding shower of sorts, but one that was not appreciated by the bridal couple or guests. A private little ceremony was held the next day in the home of Rev. Caldwell, without explosive interruptions!

In October 1953, I walked two miles out on King College Road to interview an older lady who had been present at that exciting wedding. This was Mrs. D.J. "Ella" Hart. She told me that her dress and that of her mother, the late Jane Bushong Carmack, had been badly soiled by flying sausage and broken eggs that day, and she still had the stained silk dress stashed away in a closet.

The Ebersohls left Bristol in the spring of 1884 and settled in southern Missouri. I once visited their daughter there. She gave me the picture used with this article.

THE LEGENDARY MARRYING PARSON

Much has been written concerning Alfred H. Burroughs, Bristol's legendary "marrying parson," so much so that, having a horror of historical repetition, I would not attempt another article about him had I not discovered some new information concerning his life and works.

Burroughs was born in 1833 but no one seems to know where. Early in life he married Miss Emma H. Clark. She was born in 1841 but the place is unknown as well. Burroughs later became an ordained Baptist minister and did some preaching at various places, but there is no record of him ever leading a church. It is not generally known, however, that the parson came here as a schoolteacher. We don't know exactly when he came to Bristol but it is known that, by 1871, he was teaching in the Bristol Baptist Female College. This college was located on Anderson Street where the Haven of Rest Mission now stands. At some time during the college's existence, Major Z.L. Burson was connected to it. When Burson was dismissed from what is now First Baptist Church, Rev. Burroughs sided with him. He, too, was excluded from that church on January 10, 1872. This exclusion also ended his connection with the college.

Undaunted, he then organized Burroughs High School, commonly called Bristol High School. It was in operation by August 12, 1872. Even so, low income caused this schoolmaster to go into the freight-hauling service. To do so, he was forced to borrow money from Major Burson to buy a couple of wagons and teams. He could not repay the loan. A lawsuit ensued—and so ended a beautiful friendship.

The marrying service that made him a legend in his own time began in 1879. Tennessee then had marriage laws that were rather lax. Thus, largely due to his efforts, Bristol became somewhat of a marriage mecca. He leased the famous old Nickels House Hotel and there he set up a wedding parlor and bridal suite. He would escort couples from the depot, help in securing the license, perform the ceremony and show them to the bridal suite. Sometimes the ceremony was performed right in the bridal suite. A very old lady who lived on McDowell Street who had been a maid in the hotel once showed me what remained of a lovely decorated bowl and pitcher set that had been used in this bridal suite. The chamber pot was missing. It seems that a violent fight had ensued between some newlyweds at about 2:00 a.m. During that fight, the new bride broke the chamber pot, contents and all, over the groom's head. This lady told of another time when Dr. J.F. Hicks, who lived a half block away, had to be called before daylight to deliver the new bride's baby.

In 1898, Rev. Burroughs moved his marriage works to a large house at 117 Third Street. He called this the Burroughs House. Here he not only continued to perform marriages but he also set up a sales agency for bicycles. It was here that Mrs. Burroughs died on May 19, 1906. She was buried in East Hill Cemetery in a lot that she had paid for by knitting socks that she had made for her boarders at Burroughs House.

In 1916, Rev. Burroughs, then lying sick on his death bed, married a couple that was standing before him. He died three or so hours later. The Burroughs House was still standing when I arrived in Bristol. Later, I dined several times there with friends who had a large apartment in the house. The room in which I ate was the same room where the parson had died. The house was still standing as late as 1967 but has long since been demolished.

The famed parson has been dead for over ninety years, but his memory lives on.

A Husband's Tribute

The Taj Mahal of Bristol

Extreme love for a deceased wife caused the building of the real Taj Mahal in faraway India. The same situation was behind the erection of what is certainly Bristol's largest memorial monument.

It stands in majestic splendor in a lot adjoining our local Glenwood Cemetery in Bristol, Tennessee. Hundreds view it every day from the very busy Bluff City Highway that passes nearby, but very few know the story of how it came to be.

Jane "Janie" Wood was born on March 10, 1875, in Scott County, Virginia, as a daughter of Judge Martin B. and Kate Dinwiddie Wood.

One of the most elaborate tributes to a deceased wife in the entire area is located in Glenwood Cemetery in Bristol, Tennessee. It is sometimes called the Taj Mahal of Bristol. *Courtesy of the author.*

Around 1885, her family moved to 124 Solar Street in Bristol, Virginia. She was a charming, accomplished and well-educated young woman. Many young men of the town were soon seeking her hand in marriage. Clifford Douglas Caldwell was one of them.

Caldwell was born on October 16, 1872, in Bristol, Tennessee, as a son of the Reverend George A. and Margaret Brooks Caldwell. The family lived in a grand brick house that long graced the southwest corner of Anderson and Sixth Streets. He was well educated, very intelligent, markedly kind and friendly and a rather handsome young man. Many young women of the town, seeking a handsome and provident husband, were vying for his favorable attention.

Finally, Janie Wood and Clifford Caldwell left all other suitors behind and declared their love for one another. They planned for their wedding to be held on Wednesday, October 16, 1895, in the local First Presbyterian Church. However, because her father strongly opposed the marriage, those plans were changed. Soon invitations were sent out for a party to be held in the evening of October 9, 1895, at the J.L. King home at 530 Anderson Street (the Bristol Public Library was later located in this house).

When guests arrived, they were surprised to learn that the party was actually the Caldwell–Wood wedding. Later that night, the couple left by train for a honeymoon in Atlanta, Georgia.

A few days after their marriage, the Caldwells moved to Chicago, Illinois, where Clifford soon became a very prominent businessman. This couple spent thirty-three happy years together in a luxurious apartment overlooking Lake Michigan.

Janie Wood Caldwell died in Chicago on March 10, 1923. Her body was returned to Bristol on a special train, on which rode her deeply mourning husband, and a great number of friends and business associates. Later that year, her husband erected for her a grand monument and tomb. The cost was around $20,000. On it says, "Dedicated in tenderest love to the memory of Jane Wood Caldwell by her devoted husband, December 1928."

Clifford Caldwell survived his wife by a little over twelve years. During that time, he took a second wife, Charlotte Goodlet, whom he married April 16, 1930. He died on the tenth anniversary of this second marriage, April 16, 1940. He was returned to Bristol and placed near his beloved Janie.

A Chip Saves a Woman from a Poison Cup

Again, I will here state my honest belief that if a thing can happen, it has happened in Bristol. The story that will be told here will help to establish my claim.

During the early years of Bristol, divorces were extremely hard to obtain. Adultery, desertion and extreme cruelty (usually of the life-threatening type) were the only acceptable reasons the court would consider in granting a divorce. Speedy divorce? Forget it! Often years passed before a final decree was made on a divorce petition. I will refer to this situation later.

William Benton "Ben" Shreve (he pronounced his surname as Shrevey) came to Bristol about 1875 from Bedford, Virginia, working as a section foreman on the railroad. Old timers described him as being a very large man, standing about 6½ feet tall and weighing about 250 pounds. During working hours, he was a capable, tireless and dependable railroad employee. However, when his workday was over, he sought out the excitement of old Front Street, which was then an almost unbroken line of vice dens.

Mr. Shreve did not have to travel far since, when he came to Bristol, he took up residence in the so-called Happiness Hotel that was located on that street. This was actually a combined boarding house and notorious

One of the strangest things that ever happened in Bristol was when a chipped teacup saved the life of a local woman. *Courtesy of the author.*

brothel. It was operated by a madam with an unusual but perhaps fitting name: Sweet Charity Love. Shreve claimed he was a bachelor but rumors soon followed him claiming he had been married three or four times. There was talk that he had abandoned his wife and children at some point in his past. Whatever was behind him, he soon had an unsavory reputation here of being a carousing drinker, gambler and compulsive womanizer.

This thing called love or romantic attraction can take some unusual twists. In this case, the twists were very strange.

In spite of his very unsavory reputation, Ben Shreve soon began a courtship with Miss Celia Nancy Jones, who was his exact opposite. (Perhaps opposites do attract.) She was of that elite family of Joneses who moved here from Jonesville, Virginia, and became highly respected citizens and very successful merchants.

Miss Celia, then about thirty years old, was a well-educated, refined, religious and genteel maiden lady. She was also a well-trained and practicing home nurse, and that is how she met Ben Shreve.

A close friend of Ben's was wounded in a saloon brawl and had to be cared for through a lengthy recovery in his parents' home. Miss Celia was hired to care for him. Ben often visited this friend and that is how this strange courtship began.

The town was shocked. However, that shock was mild compared to what came a little later when wedding plans were announced. Though the pastors of the mainline churches refused to marry such a mismatched couple, old major Z.L. Burson, a lay Baptist minister, did the job. The couple took up residence in the foreman's house near the depot. All seemed to go well for a while—then Ben, true to his roving nature, became keenly interested in a seventeen-year-old girl, and apparently she was keenly interested in him.

Ben consulted with a local lawyer about a speedy divorce. But, as was explained in the beginning of this article, such a thing was not to be had in Virginia at that time. It seems that he then thought of another way to be free again, and that, right quickly.

As rough a man as he was, he always prepared breakfast for him and his new bride. His practice was to put coffee on the table first, then to proceed with the cooking of the rest of the morning meal. On that particular day, he put a little special substance in the cup that he placed before Celia. He also set his own cup on the table and returned to the kitchen to bring in another course of the meal.

Fortunately, Celia was a bit fastidious. She could not stand to use a dish that was chipped or cracked—and her cup was chipped. Quietly, she switched with him. He was about to be late for work that morning so when he sat down to breakfast, he quickly emptied his coffee cup. He never went to work that morning or ever again. He soon died of the poison he had intended for his wife—all because of a chipped cup.

Well, a year or so later, Celia remarried and there was somewhat of a shock created by that wedding also. No, she didn't marry another bad character from Front Street. Indeed, her second husband was from a highly respected and affluent family. Some used an old expression that she had "robbed the cradle." She had just turned thirty-one at the time; her new husband was barely seventeen.

He was still living when I arrived in Bristol in 1953. This story and the accompanying photo came from him and his daughter, with whom he lived at the time. He always spoke fondly of the wife he almost never had.

Mason Jars, Loafers and Swift Justice

The Other Side of Bristol

Moonshine and Mountain Dew on the Streets of Bristol

Even when there were twenty-two saloons in Bristol, bootlegging was big business here. One reason for this was that the price of moonshine was always less than that charged by the legal outlets. Also, there were many seasoned drinkers who had "cut their teeth" on country-made whiskey and didn't want to change.

As one aged Bristolian said to me more than fifty years ago, "Well, son, I always bought that old mountain dew from way out yonder on Big Creek cause it had a sight more kick to it!"

Soon after it became known that I was collecting bits of local history in late 1953, I was told that I should talk to Blind Bob, who had once been one of the most notorious bootleggers in this city. He lived in one of the few remaining shacks of an area near the end of Second Street that was long known as Little Hell. It had been the home of a varied assortment of bootleggers and prostitutes for years past. The area was always dark by design. As Blind Bob put it, "We didn't want no light down here, so as soon as them city fellers put bulbs in the street lights, we shot 'em out."

Blind Bob's place had been the most patronized in that area. He sold moonshine from the shack in which he lived and he kept three or four shady ladies in a shack out back. He drew much trade because of his offering of a half pint of mountain dew and a date with one of his girls for three dollars. When I interviewed him, the shack out back had rotted away and his abode was not far from the same fate.

For several years, he had been the exclusive distributor for a moonshine operator whose still was out in the foothills of the Holston Mountain. It was hauled to Blind Bob's place in the darkness of night, well concealed under what appeared to be a wagonload of hay. But there came a time when the still was found and destroyed by officers of the law. "That put me out of business," the old bootlegger said with a long sigh.

Moonshine flowed to Bristol from the mountains a few miles from the city. Pictured here is a still located on Holston Mountain. It had been pierced by around one hundred bullets from the guns of revenue agents. *Courtesy of the author.*

He had a picture of the destroyed still, which he passed to me. He died thirteen days after my one and only interview with him. I was one of four people who were at his burial in a pauper's section of historic East Hill Cemetery.

The Big Creek Resort Bubble

Most of my older readers will have heard of the Big Creek Summer Resort, the site of which is now under the lake created by South Holston Dam. Big Creek ran down from the high mountains and emptied into the Holston River just above this dam.

The resort had its remote beginning when a mountain man from that area spent a mid-July night in the Tip Top (later Colonial) Hotel. His hotel room was so steamy hot that he felt compelled to tell how, in comparison, nights on Big

Big Creek, in the rugged mountains of Bristol, was deprived of a fine resort and hotel when a prominent Bristol businessman became concerned about his blood pressure. *Courtesy of the author.*

Creek were cool and pleasant. John R. Dickey, owner of the hotel, overheard this man's remarks. A little later, he and two or three friends went and camped on this creek just to find out if the man's claim was true. They found that his claim was correct. Dr. Dickey and his friends returned to Bristol and spread the word. In a short time, lots were laid out there and offered for sale. Several prominent Bristol families bought lots and erected summer homes upon them. In time, it became somewhat of a status symbol to be able to spend summers on Big Creek. While the fame of this resort was great, it would have been much greater had a certain scheme been brought to completion.

A man named Dr. Stanton came to Bristol from Lynchburg about 1915 and began a practice here. Though he enjoyed a modest degree of success, he still wanted to make more money. While spending a weekend at Big Creek as a guest of a local businessman, he developed a plan that he thought would bring much wealth to him and his host. The local businessman—also very fond of making money—quickly agreed to join him in the scheme. This host had shown him a large spring that flowed from under a low cliff in a little hollow near the village. Those were the days when health resorts, built around purported healing springs, were popular and enjoyed much financial success. As untrue as it was, the doctor would spread the word that he had discovered "the finest health giving spring in all the eastern United States." He would rename the Big Creek Resort as Eureka Springs. The businessman would furnish the money to build a grand resort hotel. They thought that this spa on Big Creek would become the most popular and most financially lucrative development in all of east Tennessee and southwest Virginia.

But then a little problem developed. This local businessman had high blood pressure and was being treated by the legendary Dr. Nat Dulaney. Dr. Dulaney somewhere came upon a small book that put forth a very interesting supposition as to a major cause of high blood pressure. It seems that the book put forth a theory that has had larger acceptance in recent years that telling lies would cause one's blood pressure to soar. The shrewd Dulaney, who may have had a suspicion about the entire matter, lent this book to the local businessman and that man studied it well. He knew that in the promotion of the Eureka Springs project, he was lying many times during the day and he began to fear for his life. He thought that he could tell when his blood pressure was soaring; so when he met a friend on the street, he began to tell him a big lie about the resort. He felt his blood pressure soar to such an extent that he thought he was on the verge of having a stroke. He then and there felt compelled to drop his support of the project and to further confess his wrongdoing in the whole matter. This confession caused Dr. Stanton to quickly leave town, never to be heard of again. Thus, the big Eureka Springs bubble burst. Though there would not be a grand resort and hotel, the Big Creek resort existed until the Tennessee Valley Authority flooded the area to build the dam sometime in the late 1940s.

The local businessman lived on for several years. He died in near poverty in 1944. He is buried in a barely marked grave in our own historic East Hill Cemetery. I suppose Eureka Spring still flows. If it does, it's under the deep waters of Holston Lake.

A Mayor's Swift Justice

Often I hear the complaint that present-day courts—at all levels—are too slow and easy when it comes to meting out justice. This could hardly be said of a certain Bristol case, presided over by Mayor William L. Rice in 1909. In that case, justice came in much less than an hour and was rather severe.

But before I tell the story of that trial and punishment, let us take a look at the judge on the bench when that long-remembered case was tried and its rather unusual punishment was administered.

William L. Rice was born in 1832 in Halifax County, Virginia, some two hundred miles east of Bristol. As a side note, this was the native county of Mourning Micajah Watkins, who became the wife of the Reverend James King, of local fame, on February 17, 1812. When Rice was twenty-three years old, he came to the new town of Bristol. In a very short time, he became an accepted and highly respected citizen here, so much so that he was elected as a justice of the Washington County, Virginia, Court.

When the original towns of Bristol and Goodsonville were incorporated together as the composite town of Goodson, he became acting mayor and served until Austin M. Appling was elected to that office. Later that year in 1856, he was elected to the Virginia State Legislature; it was quite an accomplishment for a young man in his midtwenties.

During the Civil War, he served in Company A of the Thirty-seventh Virginia Infantry CSA, finally reaching the rank of lieutenant. After the end of the war, he returned to Bristol.

The following years were hard economically, causing him to move to Texas where he thought he might fare better. He lived there twenty years and returned here in 1890. After returning, he established his home at 1119 West State Street. For several years, he made his living by the growing and selling of garden produce.

At the turn of the century, he decided to re-enter the field of politics. In 1902, he was elected as mayor of Bristol, Virginia, and served several terms. His office and courtroom were located in the old Virginia Courthouse in downtown Bristol. At the time, the area behind the courthouse was a notorious red-light, drinking and gambling district known as Big Hell Bottom. From that section, many a person was tried in Mayor Rice's court.

On October 2, 1909, Mayor Rice was standing in front of that courthouse when a well-known shady lady of that area came staggering along the sidewalk, cursing everyone she met. Mayor Rice took her by the arm and tried to take her into the courthouse. She jerked loose and made a dart for the Tennessee line. If she had crossed that line, she would have avoided arrest in Virginia.

Rice called out for someone to catch her and a very strong man did—Big Luke Dyer, also a resident of Big Hell Bottom. Then he carried her into the mayor's courtroom. There she continued to swear at everyone present.

Rice ordered her to be quiet. Instead she jumped up and hurled an oath right to his face. His patience broke, and he immediately broke his heavy walking cane over her head, knocking her senseless to the floor. When she finally regained her senses, he meekly went ahead with her trial and the sentence.

Not long after this incident, this lady joined a local church and became a model member. In time, she developed a strong desire to become a missionary to her own people in Africa.

Mayor Rice heard of this and offered to help raise money for her schooling and then more money for her support in the mission field. She did indeed go to the mission field and there soon married another missionary. She named her first son William Rice in honor of the man who once knocked her to the courthouse floor but later helped her become a missionary. This lady spent the rest of her life in Africa and was buried there. If anything can happen, it has happened in Bristol!

William L. Rice died in 1917 and was buried in Section 2A in Bristol's historic East Hill Cemetery.

Loafer's Glory

Occasionally in these columns I have mentioned Loafer's Glory. Some people have asked me just what and where it was. When I came to Bristol, the south side of that stretch of State Street from the railroad to Pennsylvania Avenue was—with the possible exception of one lot—solid business. For some reason, this area had become the hangout of numerous derelicts, winos and what might now be called street people. These people spent their days there loafing, drinking and begging. For all of these reasons, and perhaps more, the place became known as Loafer's Glory.

Some, if not most, alcoholics who frequented the place had reached the point where they would drink anything that contained just the slightest bit of alcohol. Cheap shaving lotion was popular with them. One business there stocked an enormous amount of this product. Shoe polish and "canned heat" were also consumed in great quantities. Somehow, they had gotten the notion that canned heat could be made harmless by soaking a dirty sock with it, then ringing it out. I have seen piles of cans and bottles, along with dirty socks, in the area behind the stores.

It was rare that one could walk through this area without being bummed for money. The plea was nearly always that a quarter was needed for a bowl of beans. As strange as it seems now, there was a café on Loafer's Glory that did sell a bowl of beans and a generous helping of cornbread for a quarter. But those in the know knew that in most cases the quarter was wanted for more drink. Once, when a beggar approached me, he made what some call a Freudian slip. "Please mister," he begged, "I need a quarter for a bowl of beer." He didn't get it!

On sunny, winter days, these people would sit on the steps of the First Baptist Church hoping to get a little warmth from the reflected heat. One day, one of the better-known inhabitants of Loafer's Glory lay back on those steps and just died. Then, later on during a summer night, another man often seen in that area, tanked up and went up to East Hill Cemetery and lay down among the graves and there died.

Two or three, of what one policeman described as fourth-class prostitutes, worked that beat. I recall that one of them was facetiously called Miss America while another was known as Shady Maye. This name wasn't given to her because she was a shady character but because she hailed from Shady Valley, Tennessee. One day, these two got into a fight over what might be called territorial rights. Shady Maye claimed that her business had greatly decreased since Miss America had appeared on the scene. Police were called, and one officer told me what a time he had trying to put them in a patrol car. He said both kicked, clawed, bit and did anything else possible to avoid being hauled to jail. He equated it to trying to put cats in water. Once in the car, they fought each other during the entire trip to the Bristol, Virginia, jail that was located on what was then Water Street. I once stood in a business place on Loafer's Glory and watched Miss America pick up a bottle, break it and, using the neck for a handle, chase a man far up Virginia Street with it. I later learned she was trying to collect a past-due bill. I have been told that her final end came in the State Hospital in Marion, Virginia, and she was buried there in the plot set aside for that purpose. Shady Maye died at the home of a sister that stood on Second High Street. (Second High was a notorious slum area of Bristol, Tennessee.)

Efforts to help these people on Loafer's Glory were usually rather futile. On a very frigid Sunday in late January 1954, I took heavy coats to three men that I had found coatless standing and shivering in front of the Interstate Hardware Building. By Wednesday all three of the men were coatless again. The coats given them had been traded for booze.

One teenager who wound up there had once been in my Sunday school class. One very cold night, this boy found a big truck parked at the curbside at the Interstate Hardware Building and used it as a shelter. He apparently was hoping to find some warmth from the engine. Lying there under that truck, he fell asleep or passed out drunk—no one knows which. Later on, when the truck moved on, the boy was crushed under the wheels. He was buried in the Potters Field section of historic East Hill Cemetery.

Eventually, most of the business houses along Loafer's Glory were torn down. The people who made it unique moved to other locations. It is no more, but my memories of it are vivid still.

The Only Legal Hanging in Bristol

Beginning during the Civil War period and extending over the following forty years or so, Bristol had several illegal hangings, or lynchings as they were commonly called. But, as best I can determine, there had been only one legal hanging here.

A family by the name of Fogarty lived near the end of what was long known as Railroad Street but was called Spencer Street when I came to Bristol. It is now Martin Luther King Boulevard. The Fogarty place was slightly south of the present-day site of the Janie Hammitt Home. In this family, there was a young girl named Annie Fogarty. In midsummer 1895, when Annie was twelve years old, she was attacked by a hired hand of the family, Kit Leftwich, who attempted to rape her. The attempt was foiled by an alert neighbor (for details of this incident, see my book "Pioneers in Paradise" page 164). He was arrested and brought to the local jail by Captain Joseph W. Owen, who had served as one of Colonel John S. Mosby's officers during the Civil War.

As news spread of the crime, a mob quickly gathered intent on another lynching. However, they were dissuaded from this rash act by Judge William F. Rhea, who promised to have Kit on the gallows within three months.

Kit's trial began in the old Bristol, Virginia, courthouse on September 9, 1895. Due to so much local prejudice, the jury was formed of men from Washington County, Virginia, instead of Bristol, Virginia. Colonel Abram Fulkerson and John S. Ashworth, both legal giants, were appointed to be counsel for the defendant. On the morning of September 11, the jury, headed by J. Stanton King from an area near Green Springs, Virginia, gave a verdict of guilty of attempted rape and fixed Kit's punishment at death by hanging.

Judge Rhea set the day of hanging to be October 11. State law then decreed that one month had to pass between the sentence and the actual execution of the prisoner. He further ordered that the prisoner be taken by John H. Gose, the town sergeant, to Lynchburg, Virginia, for safekeeping.

Near the execution date, the gallows were erected at the site of the Flat Hollow Cemetery near the present-day intersection of Buckner and Oakview Streets. The noose was ordered from a company in Cincinnati, Ohio. It had been rubbed with a substance that made it so slick that it would quickly draw tight without sticking.

Gose brought the prisoner back from Lynchburg, arriving by train just before daybreak the day of the execution. Even at that early hour, a large crowd had gathered at the depot, and, by daylight, many citizens of the town and surrounding area had gathered at the place of execution.

Annie Fogarty's father was allowed to drive the wagon that transported the prisoner to the hanging site. The prisoner was sitting on his coffin that was actually just a pine box. At around 10:00 a.m., a crowd, estimated to be about five thousand, was gathered around the execution site. This included many school children of Bristol who had been released for the purpose of impressing upon them the consequences of high crime.

Gose, executioner by reason of being the town sergeant, cut the rope holding the trap door on which the prisoner stood at 10:27 a.m. Doctors M.M. Butler and John J. Ensor pronounced the prisoner dead within a few moments of the hanging. His body was quickly buried in the Flat Hollow Cemetery. That cemetery was later moved to form the beginning of what is now known as Citizens Cemetery, located at the end of Piedmont Street. The reader may be surprised to know that the rope used for that hanging still exists and is now owned by the Bristol Historical Association.

John H. Gose (1869–1906) was only twenty-six when he served as executioner for Bristol's only legal hanging. He later long served as circuit court clerk of Bristol, Virginia.

The Women of Bristol

Nora Cross and the Devil's Hideout

Bristolians have always loved their country music. Long before the now-famous 1927 recordings that were made here in Bristol, local residents often had gatherings where mountain- and hill country-style music were greatly enjoyed.

The fiddle and the banjo seemed to be, by far, the most popular instruments used. And when these were played in that old-time style, spontaneous dancing often resulted. Usually, this was buck dancing (that is, individuals danced along following no formal rules but just jigged about as they so desired).

Some of these mountain music performers were masters of the art and would be very popular if they were living here today. Among the masters of the fiddle was Nora Cross. Some said that she was so good that her fiddling would make a preacher dance.

Cross lived somewhere in the hills north of the road that leads toward Blountville, probably in the vicinity of the headwaters of Boozy Creek. During warm weather, she usually walked barefoot the several miles into Bristol carrying her ancient and highly prized apple wood fiddle. It had belonged to her great-grandfather who had supposedly played it in the presence of George Washington at Valley Forge. Indeed, that ancestor had claimed that Washington had jigged for him when he played.

And wherever Cross took her seat to play, there were always those in attendance who could not keep from dancing. She always said that she

Nora Cross long fiddled for dances in an area of Bristol, Virginia, known as the Devil's Hideout. Then she mysteriously disappeared. *Courtesy of the author.*

couldn't play a lick unless she had her right foot free "to pat," and pat she did. And if playing in a building, she could shake the window panes with that patting foot. Her time keeping has been described as less "foot-pattin' and more foot-stompin.'"

But there wasn't much of a place downtown to dance. So a rather large platform was erected at a place near the town called the Devil's Hideout. Up where Mary Street merges with Piedmont was a shady, brush-covered area that spread around a large, rather cold spring that flowed from under the hill, about where Highland Avenue now begins. It had become a popular gathering place for the rowdies of the town to drink, gamble and tell profane stories. Often they were joined by several shady ladies of the town.

There, on weekend nights, fiddlin' Nora Cross, as she was often called, made the lively music while the rowdies, joined by some of the more respectable people of the town, danced until the wee hours of the morning. She was often assisted in this lively music making by Steve Faidley, a master of the banjo.

A supermoralist of the town, who also happened to be rather wealthy, became dismayed by the goings-on at the Devil's Hideout that he bought the site, cleaned up the land and burned the platform. No problem—the crowd just moved over to what became known as the Furnace Bottom (beyond Commonwealth near present-day Euclid Avenue, right across from present Food City). There, they built another platform and danced on.

Sometime later, probably in the late 1880s, Cross fiddled as usual to well past midnight. Then, taking her treasured fiddle under her arm, she began the long journey through the darkness to her home out in the hills.

No one ever knew what happened to her. She just simply disappeared without a trace, and no one knows her true fate to this day.

A historical note: A few years ago, a writer from New York called me and asked if I had a picture of Nora Cross. He was writing a book on musicians of the Southern Highlands. He also wanted my version of the story for inclusion in his book. I sent the picture and have been told that it has been published. I have often wondered how that writer knew of Cross and expect that it simply adds to the mystery of this old-time fiddler from the hills of Tennessee.

Annie Goforth Started Bristol's First Laundry

I largely pattern my life by a series of sayings that I try to pass on to others at every opportunity. One of those sayings is "live in hope and faith today that things will be better tomorrow." This saying came to me not from the halls of the learned but was based on a statement often made by an ex-slave laundress, Annie Goforth, who long labored here in Bristol.

Annie Goforth was born a slave on a farm on the North Fork of the Holston River about 1820. Around 1867, she arrived in Bristol. As was the lot of so many freed slaves, she had no way of making a living, but she found a way. She set up a shade tree laundry on the south bank of Beaver Creek, just below where Martin Luther King Boulevard crosses Beaver Creek. At that time, a huge spreading sycamore tree stood near the water at that location. Under this tree, she arranged her plant equipment. According to old timers, she had two or three washtubs, a large boiling pot and rub board. She also had a wooden pail for carrying water from Beaver Creek to her pots and tubs. Drying lines were stretched across the middle and back of the lot.

I was told that in the earliest years, she had a battling table. On this she spread out wet clothes, soaked them and then beat them with a heavy stick. Battling clothes was a common practice in pioneer days. She also had a battered old chair in which she sat once a day for a smoke, using an old corncob pipe. As crude as all of this seems, this was Bristol's first commercial laundry.

Laboring in humid summer heat and often standing in winter snow, she always kept her lines loaded with the town's laundry. If anyone ventured to offer sympathy for her hard lot in life, she would just shrug her shoulders and say, "Hit's a site better than diggin' in them hot fields over on the North Fork." She always kindly blessed those who passed by. "Lawd bless you suh" or "the Lawd bless you, honey," was heard by many a passerby.

In time, she became known as the Blessing Woman. As often happened, rain drenched the clothes on her lines. When that happened, she would just smile and calmly say, "No matter; the sun will shine again—it always does."

And from that statement came the foundation of one of the proverbs I live by and often share with others: "live in hope and faith today, things will be better tomorrow."

Aunt Annie saved her dimes, nickels and quarters. Finally, she was able to buy a house large enough to be used as a small boarding house. Every day at noon, she would walk half a mile from the wash place to the boarding house to "feed my people," as she would always say. Later, she built a four-room cottage to rent. I have the bill for the erection of that cottage. It came to all of $427.02. She even bought another rent house or two.

Finally, she was able to move her laundry into a small, former shoe shop on Front Street, just a few steps from her old location. There she washed clothes until she was eighty-seven years old. She then retired and lived another nine years. She died in 1916 at the age of ninety-six. She was buried in Citizens Cemetery. Even though she's been gone all these years, her words still live on.

ROSETTA'S GOLD

She was born Rosetta Hoffman in Germany about 1820. When very young, she married Samuel Lewis Beachler. (Folks in Bristol called them Bachelor, and that will be used throughout this article.) He was born January 14, 1821. This couple soon came to Baltimore, Maryland, and lived there a few years, but they were living in Fredricksburg, Virginia, when they decided to move to the new town of Bristol, Virginia–Tennessee. In early April 1855, they arrived here by stagecoach.

Rosetta Bachelor, a notorious character of early Bristol, hid a fortune in gold somewhere on the Virginia side of the 800 block of State Street. It seems that it has never been found. She is pictured here with her husband, Lewis Bachelor. *Courtesy of the author.*

Upon arrival here, they had little more than the clothes upon their backs. But they were both very industrious and applied themselves very diligently to the task of making a living. As it was, they made more than a good living. Within a few years, they had become rather wealthy. By the time Lewis died on January 3, 1876, their wealth equaled or exceeded that of the three wealthiest men in Bristol, namely J.R. Anderson, Z.L. Burson and W.W. James. Not only had they built up a huge fortune—something like $20,000 in gold—but Rosetta had gone further and become a legend in her own time. The town folks thought of her as a hard-bitten, gun-carrying, sharp-tongued, salvage woman and few dared to get her stirred up, as Ol' Dad Thomas used to say.

Lewis Bachelor died without a will. Not long after he died, a nephew began legal action to try and get part of the estate. Rosetta, who already despised that nephew, swore that he would never get a dime of it, even if she had to bury it "grave deep." And it appears that she did just that. The Bachelors never used a bank. Their wealth was always in cash, and it was generally believed that it was hidden about their home. But, with Rosetta's reputation as a trigger-happy sharpshooter and two very vicious dogs that guarded the house both day and night, nobody tried to rob or steal from her. In the dispute with her husband's nephew, she swore in court that she was a pauper, and for the next several years she lived like one. Her home quickly deteriorated and a Cherokee rose she had set during the estate dispute quickly multiplied, turning her backyard into a tangled mass of long and very thorny vines. Finally, she had moved from the old home to a little shack on Scranton Street that had formerly been one of her rent houses. The Main Street (State) house was sold and business houses were erected upon the lot. Near the end of her life, a niece, Mrs. Henry (Mary) Ruff of Catonsville, Maryland, moved the ailing Rosetta Bachelor there until her death that occurred in late June or early July 1903.

An ex-slave, Andy Susong, had long worked for Rosetta in Bristol. During the height of the dispute with her nephew, she had sent Andy to work for her twin sister, Rosanna Hoffman Naeff, in Baltimore. In 1910, Andy returned here. After making a futile search himself, he told the story that is of great interest to some this very day. On the day before Rosetta had sent him to live with her sister, she had him go to S.R. Ferguson's hardware store to buy an iron wash pot, saying that she needed a new one. Later that day, she had him dig a hole in the backyard so she could plant a Cherokee rose. Strangely, she had him dig the hole six feet deep. Her explanation was that it took such a hole to give this type of rose a good start. Next morning, he returned to find that hole had been filled within a foot of the top. She had him plant the rose, bought his ticket and sent him that day by train to her sister's home in Baltimore. He had always thought he had assisted Rosetta in burying her fortune in gold and that she wanted him out of town. And he was more convinced when, upon her deathbed, she kept muttering something about a rose bush in Bristol. Old-timers have told me that the Bachelor home was somewhere on the Virginia side of the second half of the 800 block of State Street but none of them were able to point out the exact site. Who knows, Rosetta's gold may be there probably covered by a large business.

The Quest for Rosetta's Gold

I have written of Rosetta Bachelor's gold remaining buried somewhere in the 800 block of State Street. I will now tell of a very early and certainly unusual quest for this hidden fortune. In most ways, Lewis Bachelor was the opposite of his wife. He was very quiet, humble and retired. He was thought by most folks to be rather timid with a colorless personality. He seemed to have little interest in the affairs of others. The one way he was very much like his wife was in the intense and everlasting quest for money. He became Bristol's first drayman, or freight hauler. He also opened the first bakery here that he and Rosetta largely operated at night after their daytime duties were done. He also did some carpentry work. He did about anything to add another dollar to his increasing wealth. Whereas Rosetta was greatly feared as much for her tongue as for the weapons she carried, Lewis was highly respected and admired by those who knew him. Worn out by endless toil and likely much stress, he died in his middle fifties. A great many Bristolians turned out for his funeral and followed in the great procession to the East Hill Cemetery. His funeral was conducted by the noted and early undertaker H.A. Bickley, a close friend of Lewis's who put on a grand, never-to-be-forgotten funeral. He was buried east of the western-most gate of the cemetery. As expected, soon after his death, trouble broke out about his estate. Even before that trouble developed, it became apparent that Rosetta, as a precaution, had already hidden the family fortune. Within several weeks, a few began to speculate about this supposed hidden fortune. This first speculation centered on something that happened on the day of the funeral. At the close of the funeral, Rosetta requested she be left alone with her husband's body for thirty minutes. She had closed the parlor doors but a curious lad in the crowd soon told that he had looked through a keyhole and saw Rosetta crossing the room carrying what appeared to be a very heavy bag. Then, two or three of the pallbearers said they thought the coffin was somewhat heavier when they carried it from the house than when they carried it from his bedroom into the parlor. This led to speculation that Rosetta had buried the gold with her husband. True to how speculation talk can go "had she?" soon turned into "she had!"

Then came that wet, foggy morning in early March 1876 when a man left his home in Paperville to journey into Bristol. His path lay by East Hill Cemetery—at that time it was called City Cemetery. He glanced up into the cemetery and there saw a startling sight. There was a pile of fresh dirt, and near it was a coffin turned on its side and there was a body laying face down on the wet ground. Someone had opened Lewis's grave and had gone so far as to tear the lining from the coffin in a desperate attempt at locating the gold. Was it found? Not likely. The ex-slave's story is far more plausible. My personal opinion is that it was buried beneath the rosebush that finally spread into a jungle over her backyard. We who have had experience with the Cherokee rose know that they can grow so thick that a snake can't crawl through. Later, the jungle was cleared for the erection of a business building, but I have no knowledge of the exact location.

It was Rosetta's request that her body be returned from Catonsville, Maryland, for burial at the side of her husband. For some reason, her request was not honored. She is buried in an old cemetery in Catonsville. The night after she died, a man passing East Hill Cemetery quickly ran back into town with a tale that a purple light was moving around Lewis Bachelor's grave. A couple of brave men ran up there to see for themselves. They saw the purple light circle the grave and then seemingly sink slowly into the ground. Many locals thought it was the spirit of Rosetta protesting that her request was not honored. Why purple? I have never heard of another ghost light being purple. Well, maybe Ol' Dad Thomas was right when he said "that old gal always delighted in being different!"

THE MYSTERY WOMAN OF 1900

Ol' Dad Thomas could tell you when the mystery woman appeared here. In fact, he could tell you the exact day—June 14, 1900, his wife's birthday. He had strolled down to the fruit stand near the depot to get some bananas as a gift for his wife. Knowing that the train from the south was due, he decided to see it in and see the people who were coming and going. Someone who was coming really caught his attention. A woman stepped off the train and just exuded dignity and wealth. She was dressed as if she was going for an audience with the president and had, what he described, "them glasses that hung on the nose with no hooks on 'em." And he saw her give the porter a "whole silver dollar" to carry her baggage across the street to the St. Lawrence Hotel that stood just across Front Street from the depot. (That porter usually thought himself lucky to get a quarter and usually just got a dime for the job.) Dad Thomas thought, as did many others over the next four days, that there was something strangely familiar about that mystery woman but couldn't place it.

She walked all over town, talked to many people but never revealed her name or from whence she came. Quickly she became known as the Mystery

In 1900, a spectacular mystery woman appeared in Bristol, spent a few days and then slipped away. Over eighty years passed before the mystery was solved. *Courtesy of the author.*

Woman. It was noticed that she spent much time walking up and down the Virginia side of the 400 block of Main (now State) Street. She also spent much time in front of an old frame building that then stood on the northwest corner of Lee Street and Winston's Alley. A place in the 700 block of the Tennessee side of Main Street also seemed to be of much interest to her. One day she hired a man who drove a taxi—horse and buggy type—to take her to East Hill Cemetery and told him to return for her four hours later. She carried two bouquets of flowers. Some curious person later found that one had been placed on the grave of Dr. Richard M. Coleman and the other on the grave of Lewis Bachelor. On her last day here, she spent one hour, mostly sitting silently in the sick room of an old, feeble, dope-addicted, demented woman who lived in near poverty, self-imposed as it was, on Scranton Street. It was told by this old woman's caregiver that when the mystery woman rose to leave, she embraced this old woman and weeping softly said, "Oh mother, I forgive you; I forgive you for everything you did; I forgive you all." She then placed one hundred dollars in the old woman's lap and slowly left the room. Within an hour, she boarded a southbound train never to return to Bristol again.

I cannot go into detail, but eighty-one years later, I solved the mystery. By chance, I visited an old man in central Georgia who shared with me his grandmother's handwritten memoirs. In it, Ann Bachelor Johnston described the visit to Bristol as I have written it here.

Ann Bachelor, an orphan girl, came to Bristol with her foster parents, Lewis and Rosetta Bachelor, by stagecoach in April 1855. When in her midteens, her moral laxity became so great that Rosetta Bachelor, a supermoralist, banned her from the home. Then, for a year or two, she became the surrogate wife of Dr. R.M. Coleman who lived in the 400 block of Main (State) Street. Remember how she tarried there? Remember how she placed flowers on his grave? After leaving the Coleman home, she opened Bristol's first brothel. It was located at the northwest corner of Lee Street and Winston's Alley. Remember how she lingered on the corner when she visited here? The Bachelors' first home was in the 700 block of Main (State) Street. That explains why she spent time there. And that old woman she visited on Scranton Street was her foster mother, Rosetta Bachelor.

In 1870, Ann married into a wealthy central Georgia family. There, she became a devout Methodist and spent the rest of her life as a highly respected and much beloved lady. She died on her 102nd birthday, October 28, 1944. She was the mystery lady who appeared here in June 1900. For more details concerning Ann Bachelor, see my book, *Pioneers in Paradise*, beginning on page 230.

Presidents, Jokesters, Footloose Majors and Other Characters

Bristol's Forgotten Portrait Painter

I once worked in a large antique shop that imported and sold a lot of fine portraits from England. We had a private joke in the shop of how some of our customers were buying "instant ancestors." It was true that some that bought our portraits did hang them in their homes and claimed that he or she was an affluent ancestor. Whatever the case—then or now—hand-painted portraits are often regarded as status symbols. It is mainly for that reason that they are usually rather expensive.

Before the era of photography, the only real way to preserve the image of any person was to commission an artist. The cost was prohibitive for most families, even though the work often cost less than twenty dollars through most of the early and mid-1800s. Costs varied as to degree of detail, background choices and size of image (full length, three-fourths or bust). Often, only one member of the family was chosen to have such an image made. This is why good, old portraits are now rather rare. Artists skilled in portraiture were few, thus they enjoyed considerable status in society of the time. Some of them traveled from place to place, usually lodging in the homes where they worked. Others maintained art studios. The latter usually operated in cities or larger towns.

It is not generally known that early Bristol had its own portrait painter. His name was Thomas C. Johnston. He was born in Campbell County, Virginia, in 1819. He had moved to the new town of Bristol by September of 1855.

For a few years, Bristol had her own portrait painter. He was Thomas Johnston, who is pictured here. *Courtesy of the author.*

His father, Hugh Johnston, moved here at the same time and established his home on Water Street in what is now Bristol, Virginia. The street no longer exists and was located in the general vicinity of the present Bristol, Virginia courthouse. Thomas, who must have had considerable wealth when he moved here, soon built what was long the finest house in downtown Bristol, Virginia. This house stood on the northeast corner of Main (now State) and Moore. It was of solid brick construction and was built by William Rodefer and James Fields, master builders of Abingdon, Virginia. It was the four-square design with a full English basement, essentially making a commodious house of eight large rooms. Each of them had a large fireplace. There was a Greek-revival-style portico on the front facing the street. In back was a detached kitchen and slave quarters. He had a basement art studio but also traveled to various localities in this area to work. Jonesboro, Tennessee, seems to be one of his favorite fields of labor. Provided he had known a person, Thomas Johnston could paint a good portrait from memory after that person was gone. He was much sought after for that purpose.

He and his family occupied the downtown house until 1862 when it was sold to Rev. James King. A move was then made to his father's home on Water Street. His father, Hugh, died March 19, 1874. His mother died a few years later. He continued to live there, taking care of his three maiden sisters until his death in late 1892. This early portrait painter, his wife and one or more of his children were buried in the L.F. Johnson lot, Section

1B in Bristol's historic East Hill Cemetery. Seldom ever were his works dated or signed, thus they are hard to identify. There is recollection that, to supplement his portrait painting, he also served as an ambrotypist, a form of early photography. I have the names of his several brothers and sisters and will share them with anyone who may be interested.

And what of the grand house that he built in downtown Bristol? The Kings occupied it for a few years. During their time there, the large lawn at the front was turned into a virtual rose garden. For that reason, the place became known as Roselawn. After the death of the Kings, the house became the property of their granddaughter, Charlotte "Chassie" King, who soon married Dr. A.M. Carter. Then, in 1887, Dr. Carter had the house and outbuildings demolished and erected a large business house on the site. Bricks from the older building were used in the construction of the foundation of the new building. Descendents of Chassie King Carter still own this building. It is now home to Rylands Jewelry Store and Boxwood Antiques.

Chadwick Barr Made the Dead Speak

Though he was considered to be "touched in the head" by all who knew him, and that included about everyone in the old town of Bristol, there were those who envied Chadwick Barr. For you see, this "Bristol character" of long ago spent his life mostly having fun. That may have been something to envy in a town where most men had to spend their days in dreary toil just to make a meager living.

Chadwick's parents brought him to Bristol from South Carolina when he was but a small child. His father, a railroad worker, was killed in a tragic railroad accident soon after moving here in 1877 or 1878. His widow finished raising Chadwick as best she could in a little shack in upper Buford Street near the western edge of what is now East Hill Cemetery. They were objects of charity. C.C. Campbell, who operated a large milling concern at the Goodson Street crossing of Beaver Creek, kept them in meal and flour by taking an extra toll of one pint from every run from the mill. Other kind citizens of Bristol helped them the best they could. Mrs. Barr also took in washings to help them in their meager existence.

Chadwick never went to school. He couldn't hold a job. He mostly just loafed about the town larger spending his time on Loafer's Glory (the portion of State Street between the railroad and Pennsylvania Avenue). But his mind, as weak as it may have been, wasn't idle. He was always playing a prank of

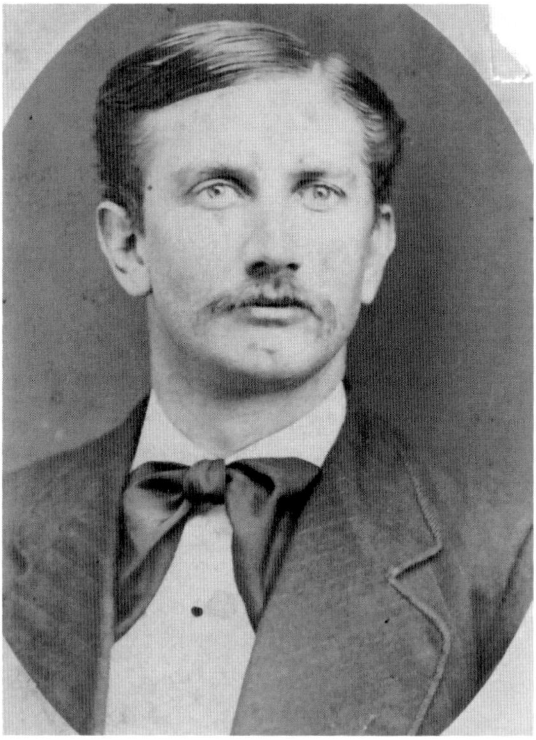

Chadwick Barr made a career of being a jokester. His most memorable joke was when he made the dead talk. *Courtesy of the author.*

some kind. By the time he reached maturity, he had considerable reputation as a practical jokester.

When I arrived in Bristol, there were a few old-timers who well remembered him and told me many stories of his pranks. They were always interesting and oftentimes hilarious. But none do I better remember than the one concerning the time he made the dead speak.

Chadwick grew up with a boy named Willis Warren. By the time Willis was twenty-one years old, he had a reputation of being one of the wildest young men in town. However, he did manage to become a carpenter working with local contractor John M. Crowell. But he soon got into trouble with the law and fled to West Virginia. A short time later, he was killed in a fight with a fellow worker. He was cut and stabbed and his throat was slashed from ear to ear. His parents had him brought back home to Bristol for burial. Some young men friends of his decided that they wanted their pictures made with him standing up under an oak tree in the family yard. Chadwick Barr was among them and, unknown to them, he had learned the art of ventriloquism. The boys had engaged Phillip Painter, who was then apprenticing under the photographer G.B. Smith, to make the picture. The men lifted the body from the coffin and as they were carrying him across the yard to the oak tree and the waiting photographer, Chadwick suddenly thought of a prank he could work on them. Willis Warren had a shrill voice that sounded much like a woman and Chadwick Barr was able to imitate that shrill and unmistakable voice. He made the corpse to cry out, "Boys, handle me a little easier. I'm still mighty sore from being cut up so bad." Well, they didn't handle him easier. They yelled out in terror, roughly dropped him to the ground and fled in all directions. Some of them didn't take time to go through the gate but jumped the fence and took off in whatever direction they faced when they hit the ground. The crowd that had gathered at the home was also terrorized. Several of the women fainted and one man in the crowd jumped backward off the porch and landed flat on his back in a rose bush! He was torn up considerably trying to free himself to run. All the while, Chadwick Barr was down rolling all over the yard in fits of hysterical laughter. If it can happen, it has happened here in Bristol.

President Andrew Johnson

He Bore the Mark of Bristol

Andrew Johnson very early formed ties to this area. In the first place, he developed a far-reaching reputation as a very capable tailor causing many in this area to seek his services. An early practice of his was to travel a very extensive circuit, taking orders and measurements for clothing, especially men's apparel. One of his principal stops was at what is now the well-known Deery Inn in Blountville. While stopping there, he became friends with Phillip Bushong, who was soon to marry Mary Elizabeth Dryden.

Johnson was engaged to make the wedding suit for this newly made friend. Not only did he make the wedding suit, he delivered it and attended the wedding. In fact, he delayed that wedding by over an hour because of his tardiness to deliver that suit.

Not long after this wedding, the Bushongs moved to Stoney Point plantation near what would become Bristol, Tennessee. This plantation became one of Johnson's stopping points on his ever-enlarging circuit. He often spent a day or two with these friends.

This friendship endured a lifetime. On Phillip Bushong's fiftieth birthday, he was given an ivory-tipped walnut walking cane by Johnson. Johnson remarked at the time that he thought it might be needed soon. In those days, fifty was thought to be the beginning of old age and decline. As it was, it was never needed; Bushong died within a short time.

However, the treasured gift from Johnson was kept in the family and passed down to later generations. It came into my hands in 1990 and is on display here at Pleasant Hill. Also kept were dishes from which Johnson ate on a later visit. They, too, are preserved to this day.

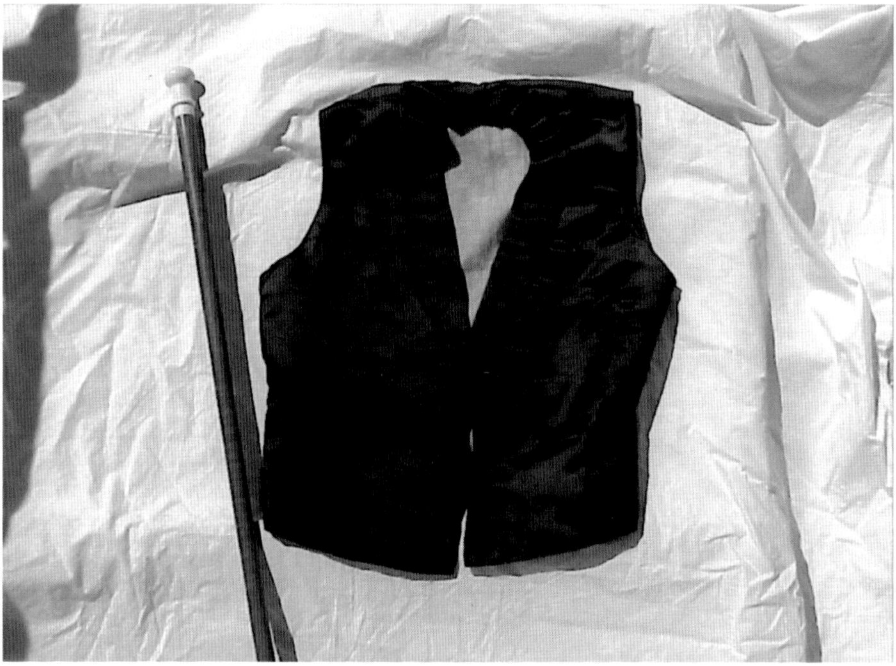

A hornet caused Andrew Johnson to suffer an injury in Bristol, the scar of which he carried the rest of his life. Pictured here is one of his walking canes and a vest he made when he was a tailor in Greeneville, Tennessee, both of which are now owned by the author. *Courtesy of the author.*

For a while, Johnson's son courted Bushong's only daughter. This courtship reached a point where marriage plans seemed to be in the making. At that point, Bushong discouraged the plans by telling his daughter that alcoholism was in the Johnson family, and he feared the marriage might lead to sorrow for her. Whatever the reason, the marriage did not take place.

At some point, on his visit to Blountville, Johnson became close friends with Joseph R. Anderson. So close were they that Johnson served as groomsman at Anderson's wedding to Malinda King on June 5, 1845. This wedding took place in the south parlor of the Reverend James King home that is now numbered 54 King Street in Bristol, Virginia. That parlor was demolished in 1892 when H.E. McCoy remodeled the house. But the fine mantel before which the wedding was performed was saved and is now in the music room of the former Margaret Mitchell home.

Johnson traveled with the newly married couple to Blountville on his way to Greeneville. They had been given a fine weight clock as a wedding present.

Neither of them knew much about such things, so it was Johnson who put the clock together, set it up and started it running. It still runs after 163 years of faithful service and was featured in a previous section of this book.

Another tie that Johnson had to Bristol was his close friendship with legendary mayor Z.L. Burson. Burson had moved to Bristol because Johnson advised him to do so, saying that he thought prospects were good for a successful future there. He was right; Burson not only became the richest man here, but he was also very influential in local civic and church affairs. He had received this advice when he went to Johnson seeking a pardon for his connection to the Confederacy. Burson always said that this advice was far more valuable to him than the pardon.

In a sense, it may be said that Johnson bore the mark of Bristol. He was injured in a stage wreck that happened at the top of the hill directly behind the new Bristol Public Library. He carried the scar of that injury to his grave.

It is noteworthy that even though Johnson was pro-Union while Bristol was pro-Confederate, there was a great celebration here in 1875 when news came that he had been elected to the U.S. Senate.

The Dancing Major

One of the best known of several legendary figures living in Bristol was Major Zachariah Lyle Burson. He was commonly known as Zach Burson. Little is known about his ancestry, except that his mother was a Jonesboro, Tennessee Lyle. (Her family was considered to be among the blue bloods of that town.) There is indication that part of his early youth was spent in Bedford County, Virginia; however, the family must have moved back to Jonesboro, for there, when still a rather young man, he married Susannah Hale, who was much younger. It has been told that there was no courtship. The two were friends and apparently liked and admired one another. It has been also told that on his twentieth birthday, Zach just decided it was time to marry, and Susannah Hale was the first girl to come to mind. He quickly went over to the Hale home and, businesslike, asked her if she would marry him. She agreed. Her family approved and they were married as soon as possible. A large family was born to them, many of them died as infants and small children, and then Susannah died fairly young. In a while, Zach married another much younger woman named Miss Nannie Baker.

Early, Zach became involved in the transportation business. At the beginning of the Civil War, his business had increased until he had a large number of

Old Major Burson danced his way out of Bristol's first Baptist church. Undaunted, he built his own church in downtown Bristol, Virginia. He is pictured here as a very young man. *Courtesy of the author.*

freight wagons operating as far north as New York and as far south as Atlanta, Georgia (his large warehouses there were destroyed in the burning of that city during the Civil War). The war broke him, but not for long. As previously stated, his longtime friend, Andrew Johnson, advised him to move to the new town of Bristol and there he could perhaps rebuild his fortune. He moved here in about 1867. Indeed, he did rebuild his fortune until he was likely the richest man in the town.

Zach became a Baptist long before he left Jonesboro; the church building in which he worshipped still stands. He also became a Baptist minister. In Bristol, he was connected with what is now the First Baptist Church, that is, for a few years. He did not believe in "closed communion" and that caused a little friction. In those days, the church could exclude any member who spoke evil of their pastor. Zach didn't like the pastor, so he did do some "evil speaking." What really brought things to a head, though, happened on a sunny afternoon in downtown Bristol.

Zach was strolling down the street when he met Caesar Susong, an ex-slave who was then eking out a living by playing old-time fiddle music for whatever coins might be given to him. Major Burson gave him a quarter; Caesar was usually lucky to just get a dime. After passing this quarter to him, Zach asked him to play a lively old tune called *Fire on the Mountain, Run Boy Run*. Caesar, so much enthused by the whole quarter that had been given him, tore into that old tune like never before.

The old major had been quite fond of dancing when younger and had engaged in many frolics where much dancing was part of the program. The first sign that he was "hearing the call of the past" was when he removed his tall top hat and began beating time on his hip. Then, in seconds, he gave a long quavering yell and began dancing circles around the old fiddler. Ol' Dad Thomas, who was standing close by, described the dance to me in February 1954, about eighty years after this event occurred. Let us hear it in his own words.

> *Why the old Major was really shavin' it down, doin' that Tennessee back step the best I ever saw as he danced circles around and around ol' Caesar Susong. Now old Big Lucy, she was a well-known wild woman who carried on her business over on Water Street, was standing by and in no time was dancing circles around ol' Caesar too! Now quite a crowd gathered up and before it was over, one of them well-known holy sisters from the Baptist Church happened to pass by. As often happens, reports of that nature become a bit distorted. Within an hour, that gal had passed to the pastor the story that ol' Major Burson had been seen downtown chasing a bad woman around and around that street fiddlin' man. It weren't no time before it became known all over town that ol' Zach Burson had danced his way out of the church.*

But, no problem. He, being tops among the richest men in town, went down on the Virginia side of Main Street and there, in the 800 block, shelled out $8,500 and built his own church—the finest building in town at the time. There were several other times in the years that followed when he again danced on the street as old Caesar Susong fiddled away.

As a final note, it is interesting to tell that the dancing major has a great-great-grandson who is now a deacon in Bristol's First Baptist Church.

Major Burson and the Watermelon Table

The legendary major Zechariah Lyle Burson of early Bristol fame left us 112 years ago, but his solid rock, outdoor watermelon table still stands. In a way, it may be considered a monument for one of the most memorable characters that has ever lived in this city.

Among the many things that has caused him to be long remembered was his voracious appetite for watermelon. In season, he sent Cedric, a former slave who had remained as a servant with his former master, downtown daily to shop among the many street peddlers for the largest melons he could find.

The old stone table on which Major Z.L. Burson cut watermelon still stands in the backyard of a fine Moore Street home in Bristol, Virginia. *Courtesy of the author.*

Cedric became a familiar sight as he trudged back up Moore Street with a couple of big melons tied in a sack and draped over his shoulder, saddle fashion. When he arrived at the Oak (name of Burson home at 342 Moore Street), the major always took time out of his busy schedule to enjoy a great feast of what he called his favorite fruit.

The four-by-nine-foot stone slab that formed the top of his melon table was found long before the Civil War, far up the side of Clinch Mountain near Mendota. It was brought down to a prosperous farm near that village where it long served as the hearth of a massive fireplace in an outside kitchen. The main house at this farm was burned during the Civil War. The place was abandoned and the remaining outside kitchen soon fell into ruins. In some manner, either by gift or purchase, Burson became owner of the stone. He had it hauled to Bristol on a four-horse freight wagon. The table was erected in the shade of the big oak that gave the place its name, the decaying stump of which still remains.

In the shade of that great oak, Burson spent many pleasant hours making good use of his unique stone table, along with family and invited friends. He once remarked that the main reason he dreaded to die was because he would have to give up his watermelon feasts. He died during the watermelon season of 1894 and now rests in the old town cemetery at Jonesborough.

Well, who knows but, somewhere out there in the great beyond, he may enjoy watermelons that taste more heavenly than those he used to enjoy around his still-standing stone table in Bristol, Virginia.

The Wild Man of Holston Mountain

When a Mrs. Cardwell went one morning to her smokehouse in the back yard of her Jacob's Creek home to get bacon for breakfast, she got more than bacon—she got the scare of her life. She had barely reached the meat bench when there suddenly sprang from behind it what she called "the most horrible creature of a man she had ever seen." He was very large, tall, had long shaggy hair and beard, fiery eyes, very large white teeth, extra large hands with dagger like fingernails and was completely nude. He jumped across the bench and over her as she fainted and fell to the floor. Her husband, who was on the back porch, saw him flee up the mountainside and into the woods. This hair-raising encounter of late December 1873 was the beginning of many tales of sightings of the legendary Wild Man of Holston Mountain.

In the late winter of 1874, a woman who lived near the head of Sharp's Creek went into the early dawning to a barn to milk her cow. She found the wild man there suckling the cow already. She immediately surrendered her rights to the milk and went screaming to the house. She would never go the barn alone after that. A year or two later, some ladies went berry pickin' on the high slopes of Holston Mountain. When they arrived at the berry patch, the dreaded wild man was already there picking berries. They gave him no competition. In record time, they arrived back home with empty buckets.

On a snowy morning in 1879, a family arose to find barefoot human tracks all around their home. There was evidence that he had tried to open the front door and he had approached several windows. That explained why the family dog had barked most of the night. Once, he quickly emptied a one-room school when he suddenly appeared at the only door. The students and teacher fled through the open windows.

Though a very fearsome sight, he was never known to hurt anyone. Some may have been hurt fleeing from him. One time, a well-known circus sent several men in the woods to try and catch him and make a side show of him. Though they had several sightings of him, they could never make a successful capture.

His range seems to have been not only a wide expanse of Holston Mountain, but there were occasional sightings of him along Holston River and far up in Shady Valley. Once he was seen in a Holston Valleyfield eating the raw corn.

He may have served two beneficial purposes. Sometimes parents brought unruly children into line by telling them that the wild man would get them if they didn't behave. And more than once, moonshiners circulated scary tales about him in an effort to keep people away from their still sites in secluded hollows.

In January 1887, some youths living near the head of Jacob's Creek were tracking rabbits in a newly fallen snow. They came upon the body of the wild man lying face downward in deep snow at the base of a cliff. It appeared that he had been running late in the night and had fallen over the cliff. He was buried where he fell. Thus ended the saga of the Wild Man of Holston Mountain, or did it? There have been numerous reports of his ghost appearing even in recent years.

Around 1900, an old ex-slave living in Bristol may have solved the mystery. He finally told that, in 1872, Big Elbert, who had been a slave of Dr. B.F. Zimmerman, Bristol's first doctor, was caught supposedly raping a white woman. Knowing that he would certainly be lynched if he were caught, he managed to flee and he had told this old ex-slave that he was going to run to the Holston Mountains, never to be back in Bristol again. He had made the statement that living in the wild would be far better than being lynched. It was widely believed that Big Elbert did indeed become the legendary Wild Man of Holston Mountain.

WILLIAM G. LINDSEY BROUGHT THE FIRST TRAIN TO BRISTOL

It is well-known that Bristol owes her existence to the coming of the railroad. It is indeed a railroad town. To be a railroad town, there must be trains. There must be engineers to operate those trains. Further, there must be an engineer who brought the first train into a town or locality. As pertains to Bristol, that honor belongs to William G. Lindsey. Mr. Lindsey had arrived at a degree of local and lasting fame when that first passenger train ground to a halt at Bristol Depot at 8:59 p.m., October 1, 1856. Though he did not know it, he had also arrived at home.

William G. Lindsey was born in Henrico County, Virginia, on Saturday, June 11, 1832. Evidently, his family moved to near Lynchburg in Campbell

County, Virginia, when he was just a small child. Very early in life, he became unhappy with his family at home and, at the age of fifteen, left to make his own way in the world. I can easily identify with him since I did the same thing at the same age. He walked into Lynchburg hoping to find employment there. Though he had not a penny in his pocket, he survived for several days by doing odd jobs for local residents, mostly for food and a night's lodging. Often the lodging consisted of a place to rest in a carriage house, basement or even a back porch or two. He often told that he went thirteen days without sleeping in a regular bed.

In 1856, William G. Lindsey, as a young man, rode into local fame by bringing the first passenger train into the new town of Bristol, Virginia–Tennessee. *Courtesy of Bob White.*

As fate would have it, he sought work in a fine home near downtown Lynchburg. When the lady of that house opened the door, she opened up a bright future for the anxious lad who stood on her porch. Being of the motherly type, she felt sympathy for the homeless boy who needed her help. She gave him a bountiful meal before assigning him to work in and about the house. That night, he slept in a regular bed in the back of that home. It so happened that the man of that house was the superintendent of the local Virginia and Tennessee Railroad shops. Over the next few days, as the boy worked about his home, he saw in the lad the capability to hire him to work as a mechanic's assistant in the railroad shops. By the time young Lindsey was eighteen, he was working as a regular mechanic and had a helper of his own. Before long, he began training as a railroad engineer. By 1856, his skill was such, as an engineer, that he was chosen to make that historic first run into Bristol.

Mr. Lindsey liked Bristol so much that he decided to make it his home. When he came here, he was twenty-four years old and unmarried. Then, on September 12, 1860, he married Rebecca Josephine Templin in Blountville, Tennessee. The ceremony was performed by Rev. John B. Logan. The certificate of their marriage still survives and is kept in an old desk here at Pleasant Hill. Soon after this marriage, the Civil War began and he enlisted in Company A of the Thirty-seventh Virginia Regiment of Confederate Soldiers. After the war ended, he served briefly as a passenger train engineer on the Bristol to Lynchburg run. Soon thereafter he became yardmaster for both Bristol railroads and served as such for twenty-five years. He then operated a plumbing business for a few years after that.

In 1868, Lindsey built a fair-sized home in an abandoned pasture of the vast Susong plantation northwest of Bristol. The rough road leading from town to this location later became a part of Lindsey Street. In 1878, he built a large two-story addition to the earlier structure. Several years ago, this house was remodeled and enclosed within brick walls. It was long known as the McChesney house. It is now the home of Mr. and Mrs. David Leonard at 711 Euclid Avenue.

Mr. Lindsey spent the last few years of his life beautifying the grounds around his home. He also did extensive railroad travel to such places as Baltimore, New York and Chicago. He then marveled at the great improvements both in the railroads and equipment since that far back time when he brought that "primitive" train winding among the hills and rolling down long valleys to Bristol on the border of Virginia and Tennessee.

William G. Lindsey died at his home January 28, 1898. He was buried in Bristol's historic East Hill Cemetery. His widow lived on for several years. She died on June 28, 1928, at 120 Johnson Street in Bristol, Virginia, and was buried at her husband's side.

THE KING OF THE BRISTOL BRICK LAYERS

John J. Fowler, who became a noted Bristol brick mason, was born to former slaves. Though he did not know the exact date, he knew that his birth occurred in April 1881. At the age of thirteen, he became a mortar mixer and carrier for John M. Crowell, a master brick maker and mason of Bristol, Virginia. Two years later, he became an apprentice of this early master brick mason.

In a short time, Mr. Crowell acknowledged that his apprentice was fast surpassing him in masonry abilities. Before he was twenty, he had gone out on his own and was fast becoming recognized as the king of Bristol bricklayers. By that time, several local contractors were hiring him to do the finish brick work on their projects.

Such was the case with the well-known E.W. King mansion on the southwest corner of Anderson and Seventh Streets. The house was built by the McCrary brothers (Samuel and James), but they hired Fowler to do the finish brick work. During that year in 1902, Fowler did the same for the Bristol depot. These two very visible jobs put him in high demand as a finish man for fine buildings.

One example of his work in downtown Bristol is the front wall of the H.P. King Building (recently Antiques Unlimited). There are three good examples within easy walking distance from my home here on Solar Hill. One is the John S. Ashworth house at 202 Johnson Street (recently Woody's House of Portraits). Another is across the street on the southwest corner of Sycamore and Johnson. This is the Bolton-Morley house, recently used as an art gallery. Then one block on the northwest corner of Solar and Sycamore is the John N. Huntsman house. Mr. Fowler did the finish work on this house in 1910. He also was the finisher on the John Mahoney house at 214 Solar Street. About 1922, Fowler built his own brick home that still stands at 326 McDowell Street.

John J. Fowler finally established his own contracting business. Though he then had other masons working under him, he still insisted on doing his own finish work. Perhaps the crown jewel of his finishing work is the main building of Sullins College.

John J. Fowler died December 21, 1927, when at the height of his building career. He was buried in the Citizens Cemetery in Bristol Virginia. Though now long dead, many examples of his masterful work remain. Even I can recognize them at a glance.

Bristol's Famous Cow

To the right of King College Road, after one passes over the Sinking Creek Bridge, is the site of old Hartfield Dairy. This long-operating dairy farm was set up by David Jenkins Hart Sr., a former Bristol merchant. The exact time this operation began is unknown but is thought to have been about 1910.

The land had been given to Mrs. Hart in 1902 by her father, Jacob Susong Carmack. Along with the dairy operation, Hart also did a considerable amount of general farming. It was his nature to excel in anything he pursued, thus he opened his dairy with the finest of registered Jersey milk cows.

A Bristol cow of Hartfield Dairy in Bristol, Tennessee, made national news as the oldest-producing Jersey milk cow in America. *Courtesy of the author.*

The dairy prospered from the start. At that time, it was the common practice of milk producers to haul their products into town in tin containers or small wooden barrels. The customers provided smaller vessels into which the milk was dipped or poured by the seller. In summer, and sometimes in winter, the streets of Bristol were often very dusty. Thus, the milk might become a little gritty as the transfer was made. For this reason, Hart began the practice of making his set-up points on side streets where the traffic was a little lighter, thus less dust. For that reason, he became known as the side street milk man.

For many years the milking of Hartfield Dairy was done by hand. The work began at 4:00 a.m., usually with the assistance of tenants kept on the farm. As the Hart children grew up, they also helped in this hand milking. The tenant house still stands across Sinking Creek from Trammel Road and back of the main house at Hartfield.

In 1912, the huge and well-constructed dairy barn was erected at Hartfield Dairy. It still stands and can be seen in the field back of the old Hart home at 2004 King College Road in Bristol, Tennessee.

During the Great Depression, milk became hard to sell. For some reason, butter sold better. So it was that Hart turned to butter making. The resultant buttermilk was sold at a rather cheap price; usually twenty-five cents per gallon. Cap Hart, a son of David, once traded a gallon of this milk for an antique hand-carved walnut comb case. It was here at Pleasant Hill but is now on display at Whispering Pines in the collection of Bob and Michelle White of Bristol, Tennessee.

At the beginning of this operation, Hart brought a prize jersey cow named Bonnie Belle Primrose. She became one of his best producers and kept right on until she became the oldest-producing registered Jersey cow in America. She became the subject of several newspaper and magazine articles. Indeed, publicity concerning her became so abundant and widespread that many visitors from near and far came to see her.

Bonnie Belle Primrose produced until she was twenty-three years old. She died at twenty-four and was buried in a ditch at the back of the Hart farm, near old Jonesborough Road. The location is within what is now Hunter Hills Circle.

David J. Hart Sr. died in 1956 and is buried in Glenwood Cemetery. His three unmarried children continued to operate Hartfield Dairy until the mid-1970s or later.

When the milking machines finally gave out, the Harts went back to milking by hand until they finally closed the operation. It was always their delight to tell me the story of Bonnie Belle Primrose, who was doubtlessly Bristol's most famous cow.

The African American Community of Bristol

Mercy Hospital Served Bristol's Black Community

Mercy Hospital was well named. It is sad but true that Bristol's earliest hospitals would not admit blacks. St. Lukes, the first large medical facility here, had as part of its charter a regulation that only whites could be admitted.

The regrettable situation, coupled with the near death of a black boy, became the main force behind the founding of Bristol's first black hospital.

There was a small settlement of blacks on Broad Street, a short distance from St. Lukes. A family named Staley briefly lived there. Their only child was a boy named Ben who was then about ten years old. Late one winter day the boy who was already sick with a cold walked home from school—almost a mile—through a cold, blowing snowstorm.

By bedtime he was deathly ill with a severe case of pneumonia, a malady that was nearly always fatal in those days. The adoring parents were desperate for help. They knew the boy could not be admitted to St. Lukes. Dr. R.B. McArthur, a black physician who had been called by the Staleys, said that if a nurse could be brought in to administer constant care, the boy might survive.

The doctor then quickly went to nearby St. Lukes to see if Miss Jen McGoldrick, manager of the hospital, might be able to suggest a nurse to help in the matter. Miss Jen was sympathetic. Being the kind lady that she was,

The first black hospital in Bristol came about by services provided for a sick youth who is pictured here after leaving Bristol and living in Fresno County, California. *Courtesy of the author.*

she was deeply grieved that the boy could not be admitted to the hospital. She then and there determined that if the boy could not be admitted, she would take the hospital to him. She gathered up essential medicines and supplies, turned the hospital over to her sister and immediately took off through the dark, snowy, frigid night to the Staley home on Broad Street. There she remained for three days and nights. She then returned to the hospital but continued to make two trips daily to check on Ben.

Dr. McArthur was also visiting the home daily. After nearly a week of intense treatment, the boy survived, never knowing that he had sparked an important conversation between his doctor and nurse. That conversation centered on the need for a black hospital in Bristol.

Dr. Alfred W. White, a black dentist, joined Dr. McArthur and Miss McGoldrick in discussion of such a hospital. Together, the three worked out details of the founding of a hospital. During those long conversations, Miss Jen often used the expression, "mercy knows no color."

In the spring of that year of 1919, a huge old unoccupied residence at 417 Garland Avenue, was leased to house the planned hospital. The dwelling was largely furnished by donations, including much surplus furniture and supplies from St. Lukes.

Inspired by Miss Jen's frequent use of the word mercy, Drs. McArthur and White chose the name Mercy Hospital. The hospital opened the day after Easter 1919.

Over the following years, Mercy Hospital faithfully served the blacks of Bristol and vicinity. Many dedicated doctors and nurses served there. It ceased to exist about 1941. Dr. McArthur left Bristol in 1925, and Dr. White lived here the rest of his life and continued to be active by serving on the board of the hospital for many years. He died in 1950 and is buried in the Citizens Cemetery.

As for Ben Staley, his family left Bristol soon after he was well and moved to Fresno County, California. They remained there as long as they lived.

SLAVE QUILT SURVIVES IN BRISTOL

The slaves who made it and long used it have been gone for more than 140 years, yet the old quilt still survives. It is rather crudely made of varying sizes of old faded pieces of wool clothing, sewn together but following no pattern or design. No one would call it beautiful. As just a quilt, it would not likely bring a dollar at a yard sale or auction. Yet it is priceless became of its unique historical connection to an era that is long past and because of it extreme rarity—rare indeed. How many do you know of in this area? How many have you seen and where would you go to find another?

Phillip Bushong and his wife, Mary Ellen Dryden Bushong, were married in 1835 and, for several years, lived in or near Blountville, Tennessee. Then they established Stoney Point plantation on what is now King College Road in Bristol, Tennessee. Their plantation house stood within a few feet of the large old brick house, erected in 1884, that is now numbered 2061 King College Road. It is currently occupied by Ann Foley. The house was a large, two-story log house that was later covered over with wood siding and a fancy portico was added at the front.

The Bushongs had four slaves. There was Martha, born July 1, 1832; her daughter Rosy, born in 1848; and Martha's much younger sister, Sarah, born about 1844. Then there was old John, born about 1828.

It is thought that all four had originally belonged to the Hammers of Paperville, who long operated the Hammer Inn in that village. According to Martha Jane Hart, a great-granddaughter of the Bushongs, these slaves

Quilts made and used by slaves are extremely rare. Only one is known to exist in Bristol and surrounding area. It is kept at historic Pleasant Hill in Bristol, Virginia. *Courtesy of the author.*

were purchased and brought to Stoney Point about the time the move was made from Blountville.

The women occupied a loft room over the kitchen while old John occupied a small log cabin in the back of the main house. Old John's cabin was taken down a few years ago by a Bushong descendant and moved to Alabama where it was re-erected.

In the mid-1850s, the slave women made the quilt pictured with this article and another very similar to it. These they filled with wool and thus had very good covers for their bed in the kitchen loft.

Martha was the family cook and housekeeper. Sarah and Rosy worked the land along with old John. Tragedy struck at Stoney Point in the spring of 1864. Rosy died on May 24 of that year and Sarah died on June 15. Martha was left alone in the loft room over the kitchen.

When the Civil War ended, Martha thought she would have to go out in the world alone to make her own way. One chilly spring morning, she came downstairs and asked Mrs. Bushong if she could take the quilts with her to make a bed wherever night may overtake her. The kind and compassionate

Mrs. Bushong told her that she would not have to leave and that she could stay on there. She went on to tell her that as long as there was food in the house, it would be shared with her.

Martha took the quilts back upstairs, very grateful for the kindness that had been shown to her. She died in that little room November 9, 1867. She was buried outside the fence of a small cemetery located near the intersection of King College and Trammel Roads. The graves of her and her relatives are not marked.

Old John did not leave such a pleasant memory. He did leave the place and found work near Bluff City. As he left, he vowed to come back and burn every building at Stoney Point. Later, someone came by and told Mrs. Bushong that she need not worry since old John had recently come down with typhoid and had died.

Phillip Bushong died on April 30, 1859, and Mrs. Bushong died on May 31, 1883. Both were buried in the Paperville Cemetery.

In 1990, the slave quilts were entrusted to me for future preservation. One was put in the Crab Orchard Museum at Tazewell, Virginia. The other is kept here at Pleasant Hill. Plans have been made for its future preservation.

OL' RAS BERRY

I never knew him; he had been gone over forty years when I arrived in Bristol. But there were several old-timers who did remember him very well. They gave me vivid accounts of his beliefs, works and practices. Though long gone, this ex-slave remains a constant inspiration to me.

He was born about 1820 in the Green Spring area of Washington County, Virginia. It is supposed that his last name—Berry—came from a pioneer family from that area. His first name was Erastus, soon shortened to Ras, thus he became Ras Berry. Even his name became a point of distinction for him.

As a youth, he came into the possession of the James family of Blountville. First as a slave, then as a hired hand, he stayed with this family for the rest of his long life. It was Ras Berry who drove the wagon bringing the W.W. James family to Bristol through the dark night after Blountville burned in 1863 during the Civil War. Soon after arriving here, Mr. James built a row of cheap rent houses at the base of Solar Hill, on the west side of what is now Piedmont Avenue. The first one built was on the southwest corner of Piedmont Avenue and Cumberland Street. This cottage, plus a garden area stretching up the hill toward the present Episcopal church, was set aside as a home for Ras Berry. A large, spreading maple tree stood at the west side of this lot in the back. This tree will figure in our story later.

Ras Berry never feared to be himself though he was very different from others. He definitely was marching to the beat of a distant drum. Perhaps his most distinguishing characteristic was in his attire. He always wore a heavy wool overcoat year-round. Several old-timers remembered seeing him labor in his garden on sultry, summer days wearing the ever-present heavy coat. Strangers in town may have been surprised to meet him on the street, walking along under a blazing sun, wearing that heavy coat. If asked about it, he would reply "what will keep out cold will keep out heat."

Ras was very much a naturalist. He believed that one should go to bed at sunset—"when God puts out the lights"—and should wake up at sunrise—"when the lights come on again." This he did religiously year in and year out. He ate only when hungry and drank only when thirsty, drinking only water his entire life. Upon rising each morning, his first act was to go stand under the huge maple tree and there loudly sing a hymn of welcome to the new day. With his loud booming voice, he could be heard over a large area of Solar Hill. This he did in all types of weather. Whether in a raging snowstorm or a balmy spring morning, he was as dependable as the crowing rooster. His usual rigorous activities continued into his ninetieth year. He had never in all his life visited a doctor and was never known to be sick a day in his life.

On a bright October morning in 1910 when the leaves of the great sugar maple were blazing red, Ras Berry began his usual morning hymn. After a line or two, he suddenly ceased. This was noticed by the nearby neighbors who went to see about him. He would never welcome another day. His life had ceased. He is buried in Citizens Cemetery at the end of Piedmont Street.

In the 1920s, James King James, who had inherited most of the W.W. James property, sold the garden and home site to developers. The Masonic temple was built on a portion of the property in 1931.

For years I have often thought that if one is to be long remembered, he or she must be different. That teaching was largely based upon Ras Berry, who gained a measure of local fame by never being afraid to be himself.

The Old Massacre Tree

I do not enjoy telling or writing this story. It is a sordid example of man's inhumanity to man. That, to me, is one of the great mysteries of life. I believe, however, dark as it is, the story must be told if for no other reason

Pictured here is the large, old sycamore tree under which a tragic massacre of ex-slaves took place. It stood until recent years. *Courtesy of the author.*

than to reflect how far we have come since those days when strong racial prejudice was so very common and often led to disastrous situations.

In those days immediately following the close of the Civil War, there were some tragic outbursts of such disastrous action in this area. One of the worst such tragedies occurred here in the summer of 1865. A reminder of that dreadful event remained until fairly recently. Columbia Street underpass carries the street of that name beneath the railroad tracks near the big curve of Martin Luther King Boulevard east of the former Douglas High School. The street crosses Beaver Creek soon after exiting the east end of that underpass. Immediately to the right of that crossing, there is a small piece of flat bottomland. There used to be a giant sycamore tree in that bottom. Soon after coming here in 1953, I visited a family who lived on Columbia Street some short distance from the great tree. On a bright, mild mid-October day, I was riding with an older co-worker to this family home when I first saw the big tree. I remarked on it and my older co-worker slowed down to let me get a good view. She then remarked she had heard her grandfather, who lived until the age of ninety-five, tell something about a massacre that took place there. She further added that he always called it the "old massacre tree" but knew no details as to why. Though she didn't know, I had already become acquainted with an old man who I felt would know. Ol' Dad Thomas, who told me so many things, did know about the tree and really opened up when asked. I can hear him now as then as he spoke on the matter.

"Dog take it, right, young-un [I was then twenty-four]. I was only eight years old but I remembered taggin' along after my Daddy and other railroad fellows up there to that place to help bury them people. They were scattered dead and lay bloody all around that big tree. I watched them fellows as they dug graves in that soft ground."

He didn't think there were ever any markers placed there. From the beginning this was a "lost cemetery."

At the close of the Civil War, many slaves were turned out to fend for themselves. Many from this area wanted to hurry south to avoid the coming cold winter and also hoped they could find a means of making a living in some way. Most followed the railroad tracks for some unknown reason. Many died of sickness or starvation. I have been told of several sites near the railroad where there are unmarked graves of these ex-slave wanderers who perished along the way.

A local man, always of an outlaw nature, served for a year or two in the Confederate army. He returned here embittered by his suffering during his tenure of service. He was seething with hatred for slaves (by then ex-slaves) who he blamed for the recent war. It was well-known that the wandering ex-slaves often stopped and rested under the big sycamore tree previously mentioned. One day, a railroad engineer pulled into town and told that he had seen a rather large group traveling along the tracks near old West Point, some distance above the sycamore. The embittered veteran heard this and quickly engaged two veterans of like mind. They hastened up the tracks. Some say they climbed the tree and hid themselves among the dense leaves. Others say they hid in the brush along the creek side. In any event, when the group arrived and sat or laid down to rest under this great spreading tree, they were immediately fired upon. In moments, ten of the eleven people lay dead or dying under the tree. A small boy of seven or eight years managed to escape and was found the next day wandering in the woods that then stretched along Beaver Creek near what is now Fairview Street. He was taken in and raised by the W.W. James family. For obvious reasons, he was always called "Lucky" James.

Ol' Dad Thomas thought the slayers left town very soon afterward but never knew anything further. The old Massacre Tree died and was taken down around 1999. Thus was lost an old Bristol landmark that carried a sad but true story.

THE INCREDIBLE JOURNEY

A journey made by a slave in 1860 is still of great inspiration to me. After the passage of nearly 150 years, I still use the story of this journey in an effort to inspire my listeners or readers to attempt things that seem to be impossible. I use it to show folks that if the desire is strong enough, seemingly unattainable goals can be attained.

Old Abe, often called Uncle Abe during his senior years, was born a slave about 1780 in what is now Floyd County, Virginia, on the plantation of Major Thomas Goodson. About 1800, he was bought by Colonel James King, who had married a daughter of this Major Goodson. He was then brought to Holly Bend on Beaver, the country estate of Colonel King in what is now Bristol. There he was trained as a gardener and beekeeper. Colonel King had a very large bee yard in his orchard above his home. This is now the site of the Ordway Cemetery.

Shortly before the death of Colonel King in 1825, Abe was brought to live on the plantation of the Colonel's son, Rev. James King. At that time, Rev. King lived on the lot that is now numbered 54 King Street in what is now Bristol, Virginia. There, Abe became the beekeeper for what his fellow slave, Si Goodson, finally made into a bee yard containing well over two hundred hives. (Both these slaves had once belonged to Major Thomas Goodson. Some of the King descendants told me long ago that Old Si was actually Abe's father.)

Abe, by his kind and faithful service, became a favorite in the Reverend King family and served them well until 1846. Then a change came. Colonel John G. English, a first cousin of Rev. King, had set up a fine plantation in Monroe County, Mississippi. He had plans to have a large bee yard on that plantation. He persuaded Rev. King to allow him to take Abe to use for a time to help with this project. It also seems that Colonel English had other plans. Before time to begin the long trip to Mississippi, he married Margaret, a daughter of Rev. King. Soon after this marriage—which occurred on September 16, 1846—the newlyweds, along with Abe and others, began the long journey to the English plantation. Some arrangements were made to keep Abe permanently on the Mississippi plantation. He served there for the next fourteen years. By that time, he was around eighty years old and had been assigned lighter work. But, Old Abe, as he was then called, had never been happy in Mississippi. As he grew older, he talked more and more of his former home far away in old Virginia. It finally became evident that his mind was becoming a bit hazy. Colonel English recorded in his diary that the old homesick slave would often stand for hours looking northeastward and muttering that he wanted to go home to old Virginia.

Then one balmy, late June night, Old Abe just disappeared. An intense search was made for him but he could never be found. A nearby stream was flooding at the time, so the conclusion was reached that he had likely tried to cross the stream and likely drowned. In early August, a letter arrived at the English home from Rev. James King, who by that time had moved to Bristol, Tennessee. The letter survives and tells the rest of the story.

"It can be hardly believed but your Abe is here. He apparently walked every mile from your place to here [Note to reader: a distance of about 450 miles]. How he found the way or escaped capture, I am unable to tell. He is completely exhausted and is sick and has a violent fever."

Yes, there are many lingering questions, even today, as to how Abe made that incredible journey. The truth is that he did. One old member of the King family told me when asked about this situation, he would simply say, "I just wanted to come here so bad, I just come on." The lesson I get from this is that strong desire and determined action can cause one to do that which might be called impossible.

Abe died three days after his arrival but left a valuable lesson for us all, a lesson that is good to this day. He was buried in a small slave cemetery that then was located on what is now the southeast corner of Rose and Seventh Streets. In the early 1870s, this cemetery was moved. Most of the bodies were taken to what was then called the Tennessee Colored Cemetery near present-day Weaver Pike. But he, along with old Si Goodson, was moved to the slave burying ground at the side of East Hill Cemetery. Silently, he rests there, but the great lesson he taught us still lives on.

Strange and Raucous Happenings

A Bizarre Death in Bristol

I long have said that if a thing can happen, it has happened in Bristol. Among those unusual happenings may be told stories of strange and bizarre deaths. One of the strangest is a story of a man who died inside the casket in which he was buried.

Many Bristolians are familiar with C.F. Gauthier and his founding of the Bristol Coffin and Casket Company. The story I will tell happened there around 1900 when the company was still located on the corner of Sycamore and Lee, in downtown Bristol, Virginia.

At the time, Mr. Gauthier only had two casket makers at work, but the time came when he needed another employee. A young man by the name of James A. Crymble had recently arrived in town from Newark, Ohio. He was a cousin to Ellis K. Crymble who for many years was a prominent Bristol citizen and had come here a few years before. James was a carpenter, and it was told that he had come to Bristol due to a building boom, knowing he would have no trouble finding work. The young man took up residence in the St. Lawrence Hotel that long stood on the northwest corner of Cumberland and Front, across for the Bristol depot. Mr. Gauthier had heard of James and, on the recommendation of his cousin, offered him a job at the casket factory.

On the day James came to work, Mr. Gauthier was not present but instructed his two older employees to show James his duties. Now both those

The man pictured here had one of the most bizarre deaths that ever occurred in Bristol. *Courtesy of the author.*

men were a bit on the prankster side so decided to do a little hazing. As soon as James arrived, he was told that in order to break into such a morbid work, he must first lie in an open casket for ten minutes. Then, the lid was to be closed over him for no more than thirty seconds. If he could endure this, he would be considered worthy to build caskets. Young James played along. A nice cherry casket had been made the day before and put in a windowless side room in back of the work area. In this he did lay the prescribed time. Then the men, assuring him that it would be opened in thirty seconds, closed and *locked* the lid over him. As they had planned, when the thirty seconds was almost up, one of them yelled, "My gosh! The locks have stuck! I can't get the lid open! What am I going to do!!"

Faintly, they heard a yell from within then all was silent. Shortly, they opened the lid. James appeared lifeless. Knowing what trouble would result the two men lifted him from the casket, carried him up near the front door and laid him face down on the floor. Then, hoping he had just fainted, one of them went running to Dr. H.B. Edmondson whose office was a block or so away at 110 Moore Street (Dr. Edmondson then lived at 221 Johnson in a house that still stands across from Pleasant Hill). The doctor hurried over and found that James A. Crymble was dead.

For the next forty years, it was believed that the man had died of a heart attack on his first day of work. Actually, he may have indeed died of a heart attack brought on by extreme panic and fright. Mr. Gauthier donated the cherry coffin in which Crymble's body was sent home for burial in Newark Ohio.

THE HOLY COW AND THE RELUCTANT ANGEL

Angel George Nickels hated his nickname, but he could never escape it. He certainly was not an angel. Indeed, he was far from it, but that is another story. I will confine this article to how he became known by the name he so hated.

George M. Nickels was a native of Nickelsville in Scott County, Virginia. Born in 1848, he joined the Confederate army when he was but sixteen years old. Soon after his war service ended, he came to Bristol where he soon became a bartender in the Nickel Plate Saloon. This saloon, located on the

George Nickels was far from being an angel but he bore the nickname Angel George for several years of his short life. *Courtesy of the author.*

northwest corner of Front and Cumberland streets, was owned by a family member, Isaac A. Nickels. The site was later occupied by the grand General Shelby Hotel.

In off hours, Nickels often did odd jobs for Capt. J.H. Wood. His connection with Captain Wood led to the situation that gave him his ill-fitting nickname.

A black woman, one Miranda Carter, had become a widow in 1871. For years she, along with her five small children, lived in a humble little cottage on upper Buford Street. She had a milk cow named Bess who provided much nourishment for her family. In those days, livestock wandered at will over the new town. One day, old Bess wandered into the Bristol railroad yard and was killed by a freight train. Captain Wood was at the depot and saw what happened. He had a special feeling for Mrs. Carter because she was once a slave on his father's plantation (old Pleasant Hill).

That night while dining at his well-supplied table, Wood decided to on a plan to help the poor woman. He remembered that a neighbor had a good milk cow for sale. George Nickels was working for him that day so he sent him to make the purchase. Now Captain Wood knew that if his act of charity became known, there would be numerous requests from others. So he told George to wait until about midnight, then lead the cow across town and place her in Miranda Carter's cow lot. He further told him that if the lady heard him and called out to simply call back that the angel of the Lord had brought her a cow from heaven.

Sure enough, the sleepless worried widow did hear strange noises in her cow lot and cried out in fear. Trying to make his voice sound heavenly, George called out the words that Captain Wood had told him then quickly fled into the darkness.

Within a day or two, Carter had spread word all over town that a fine milk cow had been delivered to her by an angel from heaven. And somehow the word leaked out that the "angel" was none other than the very unangelic George Nickels. For the rest of his short life, he was known as "Angel" George Nickels.

This heavenly gift, called the holy cow by its new owner, Mrs. Carter, became the best-known milk producer in Bristol. Meanwhile, the "angel" continued to build his reputation as an avid gambler, loan shark, bartender and persistent womanizer.

In 1885, he "stole" the second wife of his boss, Isaac A. Nickels, and fled to Montgomery, Alabama. There he contracted some type of a wasting disease. The woman deserted him and left with another man. Near Christmas that same year, very sick and destitute, he managed to return to Bristol.

Here he was taken in and cared for by his former boss whose wife had been stolen. He died in a little room in the back of the Nickel Plate Saloon on January 3, 1886. He was buried in the Nickels family lot in our historic East Hill Cemetery.

A Mouse Enlivens the Church Service

Striptease acts and nude dancing are not usually part of church services. But there was a bright Sunday morning back there in June 1886 when such happened in Bristol's Central Presbyterian Church.

In defense of that great and still existing church, I will say that the show was not a part of the planned program. Indeed, it was such a sudden shock and surprise that several of the more prudish women in the congregation quickly fainted.

For several years after this church was founded, a small pedal-type organ was its sole source of music. Then around 1885, Colonel John G. English, who was one of the wealthier members of this church, donated a much larger and finer organ. Perhaps the fact that his daughter, Jeannie Morgain English, had become the church organist was the inspiration for this gift. Colonel English was very proud of her musical ability and delighted to hear her play.

This larger organ was not the pedal type. Instead, it had a hand pump at the back that required a rather strong pumper to keep the air flowing steadily through long and usually slow Presbyterian hymns. At first the church tried a system of volunteers for this task of pumping. That did not work out so well. Soon a rather muscular youth, one Judson Meek, was hired to do this at a pay rate of four dollars per month. Judson, then about seventeen years old, was from a rather poor family who lived on Burson Row, a notorious slum section near present day Quarry Street.

Near service time, he would slip in a side door near the large organ, kneel to the job and then quickly slip out when his job was done. Thus, most of the congregation had never seen the organ pumper until that certain June morning in 1886.

During the singing of the first hymn on that morning, the music suddenly ceased, as did the singing. But the sanctuary was not silent. From behind the organ came kicking, knocking jumping sounds, accompanied by screams and yells and unholy curses. A mouse running across the floor had entered Judson's open pant leg and was rapidly scratching its way upward.

A mouse caused a striptease show to occur in old Central Presbyterian Church in Bristol, Virginia. *Courtesy of the author.*

In moments, the terrorized lad jumped from behind the organ, doing a wild, knocking dance of sorts. Beside himself with fear, he stripped his pants off, threw them high in the air and continued his frantic knocking dance. Now, as it was with most poor boys of that time, he wore no underwear. Shall we say then that the first view many of the congregation had of their organ pumper was complete and unobstructed. Perhaps the view for some was brief. At least it is known that a mother, sitting on the front pew, slammed a fan over her daughter's eyes—quick thinking wouldn't you say!

Fortunately, the frenzied lad soon regained a measure of sanity, leaped out the side door and raced up Moore Street toward home. One wonders if there was a volunteer to pump the organ for the rest of the service or if in fact the service continued at all!

But continued or not, it is certain that the service, or part thereof, was long remembered by the folks at Central Presbyterian.

Judson Meek was fined five dollars (suspended) for indecent exposure, disturbing public worship and uttering profane and blasphemous in public. He soon left Bristol and finally settled in Mississippi.

Familiar Places with Hidden Faces

Solar Hill Revisited

Now that much restoration work has been done on Bristol's historic Solar Hill, I think it is a good time to review the history of this section of our city. This area was formerly known as part of King's Meadows, usually referred to as the Upper Meadows. Later, it became Lancaster Hill, so named for Thomas C. Lancaster who bought and occupied the old James King house for some time. Then, because of an observatory set up on the hill to view the Great Eclipse of August 7, 1869, this became known as Solar Hill (it is interesting to note that this year marks the 140th anniversary of the event). I might mention here as a side note of interest that my great-grandfather Boggs died in Letcher County, Kentucky, during that eclipse. Some thought this darkness that fell over the hills and mountains of Kentucky meant that my ancestor was doomed eternally but we would not think such things now. This area known as Solar Hill is part of the old Sapling Grove tract. Earlier, it was owned by the estate of General Evan Shelby. In 1814, it came into the ownership of the pioneer King family. The Reverend James King was living on it by 1817 when his third son, Cyrus King, was born. It was Rev. King's slaves that cleared the hill and this became his milk cow pasture. Those cows had a habit of gathering about noon every day in a grove of huge oak trees that had been left when the hill was cleared. This became known as the Noon Grove. This noted grove was located on and around what is now the northwest corner of Solar and Cumberland Streets.

A rural Washington County Virginia post office was established in the King home in 1839 that was known as Sapling Grove. At that time, a change was made in the Old Stage Road to serve this post office. The route of that road is now Kings Alley and King Street. It passed by what was then the backyard of the King home, but this soon became the front yard.

In June 1853, Rev. King and family left the hill and moved to a house that he had built on Beaver Creek near what is now the Melrose Street Bridge. The Sapling Grove Post Office, that then had Campbell Galliher as postmaster, was discontinued on October 1, 1853. The new Bristol Post Office was then established on the following November 5, 1853. The last run of the stagecoach across Solar Hill was made at about 1:00 p.m. October 28, 1856. By 1860, the Solar Hill lands had become the property of Joseph Johnston of Philadelphia, Pennsylvania.

Soon after the close of the Civil War, it became apparent that if Bristol were to grow, more land would have to be made available for development. At first, Captain J.H. Wood, who built my home, Pleasant Hill, and his father-in-law, W.W. James, sought to buy the land and make a private development of it. The plan was abandoned because of financial difficulties incurred by Mr. James. However, J.H. Wood headed the move to have the town buy the land. A deal was made with Johnston to purchase the land for $24,937.50. The town approved the purchase by a vote of 101 to 21. Mayor I.C. Fowler, John H. Winston and Captain Joseph W. Owen directed the laying out and naming of the streets. The sale of lots was set for July 5, 1871. On that day, David Sullins, for whom Sullins College was later named, rode a horse named Prince as he moved from lot to lot making the sales. Two lads, Frank Winston and a Pepper boy, went ahead of Sullins flagging the lots.

The first lot sold was on the southwest corner of King and Sullins Streets (behind our present public library). It was sold to Nathan Dodd for $300. The lot that brought the most money was located on the southwest corner of Johnson and Scott Streets. It was bought my Mr. McCormick for $605. The fact that it sold for more than other lots that had much better views may be explained by its fronting on a planned railroad. In those days, having a residence in close view of a railroad was considered to be somewhat of a status symbol. The two first houses completed after the sale included the W.W. James house on Sullins Street and the G.M. Whitten house on 203 Solar. This house was later known as the Wallace house and even later as the Johnson house. The Whitten–Wallace–Johnson house still stands. Solar Hill was long the most elite section of Bristol, Virginia. It has now become an official historic district and is making a comeback with much restoration being done.

The Prophecy of Cedar Hill

David King Sr. came from Pennsylvania to what is now Sullivan County, Tennessee (it was then a part of North Carolina) when he was fifteen years old. He came working as a driver for John Sharpe, a pioneer settler of the area. Somewhere far up in the Shenandoah Valley, a camp for the night was made.

While sleeping under the stars there the lad had what he later would call a vivid, prophetic dream. In that dream, he saw a low hill covered by gnarled old cedar trees. A voice in that dream told him that someday that hill would be his home-site in the new country to which he was going. At that time, he thought little of the strange dream.

Once David King was here, John Sharpe urged the lad to stay with him. As an inducement, he offered to give him any one of his nine daughters as a wife. Further, he would give the couple a square mile of his land for a future home.

The site for Cedar Hill and its name came in the form of a prophetic dream. *Courtesy of the author.*

Young David accepted the offer. Strangely, he chose Elizabeth Sharpe, who was then only six years old. This meant that he would have to wait ten years until she became sixteen before the marriage could take place. They were married a few days after she reached that age.

When the land was being surveyed for their new estate, David King found the cedar-covered hill that he had seen in his dream. He felt that this was the place for his new home. In 1791, David King built a two-pen log house with open hall between them, at that location. He called the new home Cedar Hill. There, fourteen children were born to the couple. Hundreds of people in this location and elsewhere descend from this large family.

In 1846, a son in this family, David O. King, tore away one of the log pens and added a two-story house to what remained. The former open hall became the present dining room. The other pen became the kitchen and remains to this day. The house is five years older than the state of Tennessee. Theodore Roosevelt spent a night or two at Cedar Hill when he was gathering information for his historical work, *The Winning of the West*.

The house was owned for several years by the Painter family, descendants of David King. Thus it became known as Painter Place. It is located about seven miles from Bristol on Painter Creek Road in Holston Valley. The Tennessee–Virginia state line passes within three feet of the front porch. It is now owned by King College.

FAREWELL TO STRAWBERRY FIELD

It is not generally known that the Bristol Depot, that has been recently so well restored, stands on what was once a large wild strawberry field. Malinda King Anderson, a daughter of Rev. James King, who was born and reared on the vast King plantation, well remembered and often spoke of this beautiful field. In season, it made a splash of red in the midst of the green King meadows. These berries grew in such profuse abundance that the hoofs of horses and cattle would become as red as if painted.

The King's Meadows began just back of the First Baptist Church and extended westward across the Beaver Flats and then upward to include Solar Hill to about Oak Street. The latter section was known as the Upper Meadows. The portion of the meadows that became downtown Bristol and four acres beyond the depot lot were sold to Joseph R. Anderson in 1852 and upon these acres he laid out the original town of Bristol.

The erection of the Bristol Depot and other railroad buildings destroyed one of the two largest natural wild strawberry fields in southwest Virginia. *Courtesy of Bob White.*

Just why such a large field of strawberries developed in the midst of King's Meadows, no one could tell. A similar field existed in Strawberry Plains, Tennessee. Strangely, that field belonged to the only sister of Rev. James King, Sarah King Williams. When the route of the Virginia and Tennessee Railroad was finally determined, it lay directly through this field of wild strawberries. This route left the Goodson lands at Beaver Creek and then proceeded through the strawberry fields extending twelve hundred feet to within five feet of the state line.

It was then that Rev. King generously donated a tract of land for the terminal depot. This lot began at the state line and extended northward to join the Goodson land at Beaver Creek. It was roughly bounded on the north by present Washington Street and on the south of what is now Martin Luther King Boulevard (formerly old Front Street). This depot lot took in virtually all the old wild strawberry field. It should be pointed out that a large spring flowed from the bank a few feet from the west door of the depot. It was called the Strawberry Spring. Joseph Anderson planned to build his home just across from this spring but finally chose the lot that is now the southwest corner of State and Martin Luther King Boulevard.

The building of this first depot and the laying of the rails plus a wood yard (the train engines were then fired by wood) destroyed much of the wild strawberry field. Soon after the first depot was built, three or four houses built for railroad employees—sometimes called section houses—were built near the Beaver Creek crossing of Washington Street. This destroyed more of the strawberry field. Then in 1881, a large freight station was built. This covered much of the remaining area where the wild strawberries so profusely grew. As the succeeding three stations were built, each became larger and thus, more and more of the old field was covered.

There is much evidence that small strawberry plants sprung up in other parts of King's Meadows. Mrs. Joseph Anderson once told that her husband, while showing a town lot that he had for sale on Lee Street, found a small cluster of these berries still growing. He pulled them up, brought them home to his new residence at 516 Anderson Street and there had them planted as a reminder of the once large field of them on the depot lot. They remained in that yard for years. The late Margaret Anderson Piper, a granddaughter of Joseph Anderson, remembered seeing them there. As I walked across the northern portion of the depot lot in the spring of 1956, I came upon a cluster of wild strawberries. I still think they were a remnant of the old wild strawberry field.

THE HISTORY OF THE MYSTERIOUS LOT

As one crosses the railroad, going eastward on State Street, one may notice that there is a large, vacant lot to the south—or the right—of that street. Various times, I have been asked about what some called "the mysterious lot." The purpose of this article is to answer that question.

As far as can be determined, that lot has been vacant for about 130 years. Originally, this lot was encompassed within the vast plantation of Rev. James King. Before the late 1840s, it was part of one of his large cornfields. Hattie King Taylor, a granddaughter of Rev. King, wrote that this field was used by Rev. King to plant his yellow corn. It seems that he grew a special kind of yellow corn because his family liked bread made from this type of cornmeal and so he always reserved this especially rich part of his plantation for that purpose. This situation existed for several years then the rail survey for the East Tennessee and Virginia Railroad was made. The Virginia and Tennessee survey had also been made and even though these rail lines would not be joined for several years, they would form a long northeast and southwest corridor. It was virtually certain that a town would develop at the point where these two very important railroads met. Rev. King had land extending well into Virginia ending at Beaver Creek, thus he had the grand opportunity of becoming the founder of a town that would be in two states. According to his daughter, Mrs. Malinda King Anderson, he had originally planned to be the founder of what later became Bristol, Tennessee and Virginia, but for certain reasons he chose not to do this. Instead, he chose to pass that honor on to his son-in-law, Joseph Rhea Anderson, and the land was sold to him for the "two state" development. Rev. King did donate land to be used for depot sites for both railroads. The aforementioned vacant lot is the land that he gave for the East Tennessee and Virginia Railroad for the depot site.

As was the case on the Virginia side of Bristol, the Tennessee depot was constructed before the rails were actually laid. By the summer of 1857, this depot had been put under roof. At that time, there was a broad lawn between the west side of Third Street and the depot. Children of that area played ball there and the unfinished building was used as a meeting hall for local residents. At one time, Andrew Johnson drew a large crowd to hear him speak there. There were not many Bristolians residing here at that time, but folks also came from the surrounding area to the new town. There is also mention of a play being put on in this depot.

The rails were laid in 1858 and it was then the depot began its intended usage. But then came the Civil War. During this destructive conflict, this depot was burned. There is a myth in Bristol history that it was never rebuilt, but it was. Here is a good place to be warned that there are many myths in Bristol history. It is wise to check things carefully before one writes or speaks on this subject.

The rails had not been joined with the Virginia and Tennessee Railroad so it was needful that there would be a building in which to conduct local business. I have seen this railroad's advertisement seeking bids for the construction of a new depot. According to information obtained through various sources, George W. Blackley, a master carpenter, contracted to build this new depot. The cost is unknown. It is known, however, that it was of frame construction using rather large timbers that came from Morgan's Saw Mill then located near the junction of Williams and Washington Streets. It is also known that it was painted a dull, rustic brown. Ol' Dad Thomas confirmed this after I was told the story by two or three other older Bristolians.

This building served until 1878 when the two railroads were finally joined at Bristol. The late James King Brewer said he was about sixteen when he helped dismantle the old building. He was born in 1864, so this would place the approximate date of the demolishing of this old Bristol landmark to about 1880. He also helped haul the timbers to a lot on the south side of the 400 block of Main (now State) Street. Joseph R. Anderson had bought the depot and he used the timbers in the construction of a three-story building that he erected in 1881 on the lot that is now numbered 410 State. This was the building in which the "big bang" of country music occurred in 1927. The building was destroyed by fire in February 1949, thus the last remnants of the Tennessee Depot were lost forever.

THE CHRISTMAS GIFT HOUSE

On Christmas Eve about 1895, a lady who had never been to Bristol before, arrived at the local train station. Soon after arriving, she was presented with a Christmas present that was beyond belief.

The story begins with the great timber boom that began shortly before 1900 and continued several years thereafter. In her early years, the fast-

Coming to join her husband in Bristol, Mrs. A.F. Willey found a new and well-furnished house waiting. It was her special Christmas gift and one she never forgot. *Courtesy of the author.*

growing town of Bristol's demand for lumber was filled by saw mills located at various points nearby. A few Bristol mills obtained the saw logs from area forests. It was long known that the Holston and adjoining mountains nearby were covered with fine, virgin timber. However, this valuable source of building materials had not been really tapped into until the timber boom came. Perhaps the distance and difficulty of logging the rough terrain caused the delay. But soon a few enterprising businessmen from out of state began to come in and overcame the obstacles that had delayed the removal of this timber. They had plans to obtain lumber, not only for building purposes here locally but also had plans to ship it—in great quantities—to distant points.

Among those enterprising men was Allison F. Willey. At first, he set up his lumber works in Bluff City where he built a boom in the Holston River to catch the logs that had been cut on the mountains and floated down the river. But a dispute arose with the town fathers of Bluff City. This led to his removing his works to Bristol. Here he joined with Constantine Morton and Everett P. Lewis to form the firm of Morton Lewis and Willey Lumber Company of which he served as general manager for several years. This company operated the Holston Valley Railroad for the purpose of bringing logs from the mountains to the processing plant that was located near the end of Georgia Avenue. The Cortrim Lumber Company later occupied this site until a burn out in recent years. (The Willey Boom section of Bristol was named for Mr. Willey.) Over the next few years, Mr. Willey saved choice lumber from this plant with the intention of putting it into a fine home he would build at a later date. He also chose choice walnut and cherry lumber and shipped that to a furniture factory in Grand Rapids, Michigan, to be made into fine furniture for this fine home.

In the autumn of 1953, the late Mrs. Sam Scott—affectionately known to everyone as Aunt Betty—sat by the fireside in her humble home on Second High Street and told me the rest of the story. She said that Mr. Willey finally built his fine late Victorian home at 420 Pennsylvania Avenue. This would be the northwest corner of Pennsylvania Avenue and Ash Street. He had it all decorated and completely furnished without the knowledge of his wife. Then he sent for her. She was scheduled to arrive late in the afternoon of Christmas Eve. He met her at the local depot and brought her, in his carriage, to the new home he had built for her. This was the first she knew of it, and what a surprise it was! It was a great Christmas gift indeed. He had also hired Aunt Betty Scott to have supper cooked and on the table awaiting them when they arrived from the depot. Indeed, it was a great surprise and joy to his wife Hattie Willey. It was the kind of gift that few people would ever receive.

Aunt Betty, with moist eyes, told how Mrs. Willey was so excited she could hardly eat supper. Then, as quickly as the meal was over, she wandered from room to room, again and again, to view the beautifully decorated walls, the fine hanging oil lamps and the beautiful furniture from Grand Rapids that had been made especially for the house, all made from the choice timber harvested from the Holston Mountains.

The Willeys enjoyed their home for a few years and then other business interests caused them to move on. After they left the house, several different families lived there. For a few years, it served as the parsonage of the First Baptist Church. It is known that Rev. J. Emmerson Hicks, pastor of this church, lived there during the 1938–40 period. As the years passed, it became an apartment house and fell on hard times, so much so that it became necessary to demolish it. I was made very sad when one day I drove out Pennsylvania and saw it had been demolished. But the lumber had been neatly stacked on the lot and people came from near and far to admire the quality of the lumber that had been cut on Holston Mountain, processed in the Willey mills and made into such a beautiful home.

Perhaps it is fitting that the site of this Christmas gift house was later turned into a flower garden for the Vince Kinsler home that occupies the lot next door.

About the Author

Bud Phillips has been a resident of Bristol, Virginia, since 1953. He first began to hear strange and unique stories about the past from his older clients when he served as a social worker. In March 2006, he began writing a history column for the sesquicentennial celebrations of Bristol, and due to popular demand, he continues to write for the *Bristol Herald Courier* to this day.